Marquetry Techniques

Marquetry Techniques

Colin Holcombe

The Crowood Press

First Published in 1997 by
The Crowood Press Ltd
Ramsbury, Marlborough
Wiltshire SN8 2HR

British Library Cataloguing-in-Publication Data
A catalogue reference for this book is available from the British
Library.

ISBN 1 86126 057 1

Line illustrations by Andrew Green.
Photographs by the author and Dave Hartnell.

Photograph previous page: French marquetry cabinet, c.1865.

Dedication
I should like to dedicate this book to my wife Eileen for putting
up with me for twenty-five years, and to the memory of a dear
friend, John Cambridge 1951–96.

All materials, tools, veneers and kits for both the beginner
and the more experienced marqueteer can be obtained from:
The Art Veneer Co. Ltd, Chiswick Avenue Industrial Estate,
Mildenhall, Suffolk LP28 7AY.

Typefaces used: text, New Baskerville and Garamond; headings,
Optima Bold.

Typeset and designed by
D & N Publishing
Membury Business Park, Lambourn Woodlands
Hungerford, Berkshire.

Printed and bound by Paramount Printing Ltd, Hong Kong.

CONTENTS

ACKNOWLEDGEMENTS

I should like to acknowledge the skill and artistry of: F. L. Holmes for 'John Major'; F. E. Kerridge for 'New Hampshire Fall'; W. A. Maestranzi for 'Spirit of the Trees'; Andrew Smith for 'The Pink Bonnet'; Eddey Stevens for 'In a Position to Know'; and Pauline Stevens for 'Lilies'.

FURNITURE
Regency centre table in the seventeenth-century style (page 8) courtesy of Lewis & Lloyd Antiques, London; piano, c.1785 (page 16) courtesy of Bruno Cooper, Norfolk; Victorian credenza (page 41) courtesy of P. R. Barham, London; William and Mary secretaire (page 9) courtesy of Dench Antiques, Kent; ivory toilet mirror (page 75) courtesy of Richard Miles, Fine Art; French marquetry cabinet, c.1865 (page 2) courtesy of David H. Dickinson Ltd, Cheshire; William and Mary chest of drawers (page 49) courtesy of Market House Antiques, Norfolk.

Marquetry is the art of making patterns and pictures by cutting out the various pieces required and assembling them with glue on to a ground panel or piece of furniture. The most common material used in the making of marquetry is wood, but wooden veneers are by no means exclusive: tortoiseshell, ivory, mother-of-pearl and metals such as brass, pewter, gold and silver have all been used to great effect over the years. A close-up (overleaf) of the top of the beautiful Regency table made in the Louis XIV style illustrates how ivory has been used to great effect in conjunction with wood veneers.

Marquetry covers a huge range as far as standards and levels of skill are concerned, ranging from the beginner's first attempt at a simple design purchased as a kit, through the more advance examples of the experienced marquetarian, who draws his own designs and shades and colours his veneers, perhaps producing a piece of work to rival that of any painting, to the works of art produced by the French and English cabinet-makers of the seventeenth and eighteenth centuries.

There is no reason why today's beginner, given patience and practice should not produce a work worthy of comparison with the very best; but even if one is not destined to produce a work of art, marquetry can and does give an immense amount of pleasure and personal satisfaction.

The origins of marquetry date back to Roman times, but then it consisted more of what we would now call inlay. Pieces of thick, hand-cut veneer would be let into cavities created in the surface of solid wood to form a decoration. It was probably in Italy that the technique of completely covering the surface to be decorated with the assembled pieces, rather than inlaying them, was developed.

During the fourteenth and fifteenth centuries, both marquetry and what we today refer to as parquetry, was practised in Italy, and evolved through the Florentine school of marquetry with the use of perspective and pictorial effects; indeed some would argue that Benedetto da Maiano (AD1444–1496), of the Florentine school, was the man who invented marquetry as we know it. It was also during this period and in the early sixteenth century that wood first started to be dyed and shaded by the use of heat.

During the seventeenth century German marquetry-cutters came up with the idea of placing veneers of different woods one on top of the other and cutting out a pattern from the assembled stack. These pieces of veneer, when cut, could then be assembled to make up a pattern, the simple interchange technique. This technique was adopted and developed in the seventeenth century by probably the most famous name in marquetry, André Charles Boulle (AD1642–1732), who was cabinet-maker to Louis XIV of France. Boulle produced some of the most beautiful pieces of furniture in the world, including much of the furniture at Versailles. Today he is probably best remembered for his tortoiseshell and brass interchange marquetry – so much so, that today any marquetry made up of tortoiseshell and brass in this way is referred to as Boulle work. Boulle would cut his designs from sheets of brass and tortoiseshell, held together so that background and design could be cut in one operation. After separation, the brass would then fit neatly into the tortoiseshell to form a very striking design. The waste sheets, of course, would also then fit one into the other to form another pattern, one comprising of a

A seventeenth-century style centre table made during the Regency period and showing how different materials, such as ivory, as well as different woods can be combined to form beautiful marquetry.

Close-up of the above table showing the wood and ivory veneer.

A fine William and Mary walnut secretaire, English, c.1690, with oyster veneers and marquetry panels.

Close-up of the front of the secretaire.

tortoiseshell design on a brass background. In this way a pair of very beautiful and yet quite different cabinets would be produced, each being the counter-image of the other, and so these pieces are known as Boulle and Counter-Boulle.

Before the introduction of machinery, all veneers were cut with a handsaw. Later the saws were driven by steam or water, but it would not have been possible to produce more than five or six sheets from an inch-thick board – the saw would have destroyed as much timber as would have been cut into veneers. Any marquetry pattern cut from these veneers which would be much too thick to cut with a knife, would need to be cut with a fretsaw, and this was done on the marquetry-cutter's 'donkey'. The donkey is a seat or bench, having a vice or clamp at one end to hold the veneers that were being cut. The vice was operated by the marquetry-cutter's foot on a pedal and in this way the work could be quickly released, turned and reclamped in the vice. The saw that held the marquetry-

cutting blade was mounted horizontally on the donkey and was operated backwards and forwards by hand. Operating the saw with one hand, the vice by foot and feeding the veneers into the saw with the other hand would have required a great deal of skill and experience.

In 1809 knife-cut softwoods became available, but it was not until 1875 that hardwoods could be cut in this way. These days the marquetarian has the opportunity of using veneers that are knife-cut very thinly, and it is possible for the marquetry-cutter to cut his pattern from single sheets of veneer with a craft knife or scalpel. There are advantages to both knife- and saw-cut methods of marquetry, depending on the result you require. If, for instance, you have a large number of the same panels to produce, or if you are repairing or reproducing an antique panel, then it would obviously be advantageous to use the fretsaw, as it is possible to make up a sandwich of veneers and cut a large number in one go. Another reason for using a saw might be the fact that some veneers are quite difficult to cut with a knife, either because of the grain or because the veneers themselves have been saw-cut and are quite thick. On the other hand, if the picture is a one-off, or if the direction of grain for various elements in your picture is important, it may well be far easier if you use the window method and knife-cut your design, so that you can view the grain through the window before you cut and in this way select the very best section of grain for your purpose. Whichever method you choose – and there is no reason, by the way, why both can't be used on the same picture – and however far you eventually go with your marquetry, I wish you every success, and I hope you will find this book an invaluable and constant source of information.

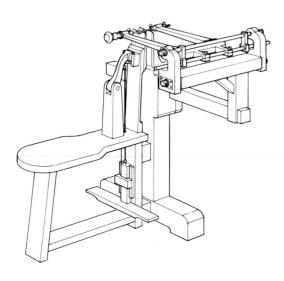

Fig 1 The marquetry cutter's 'Donkey'.

one

KNIFE-CUT MARQUETRY

THE TOOLS

THE KNIFE

It is difficult to give much advice on the choice of knife, as what may suit one person will not necessarily suit another. Some people use a surgeon's scalpel, but these leave a lot of the blade exposed and this can cause it to break when pressure is applied. There are various craft knives on the market, some of which will hold the scalpel blade far better than a scalpel for the purposes of marquetry. Some have a sectional blade, so that when it becomes blunt you simply snap off the end and start again with a new sharp section. The best advice I can give is to try a few different knives to see which one feels the most comfortable. Select a knife that is comfortable in the hand and one that has a thin blade, but not too flexible, as a flexible blade will tend to wander off course easily.

SHARPENING STONE

An oilstone of some kind should always be on hand for sharpening your knife. A two-sided carborundum is useful, or you may be able to get hold of a Japanese water stone, which will give you a really fine edge. There are two ways in which a knife blade can be sharpened: either you can sharpen it in what might be regarded as the conventional way, by honing the bevels on each side of the blade, in which case the Japanese stone will be a good investment, or, as many marquetarians do, you can hone away the back edge of the blade, and because it

is only the tip of the blade that is used in cutting, a new unused and sharp section of blade will come into use (*see* page 12).

CUTTING BOARD

Some people like to cut their veneers on a piece of wood or MDF board, others on thick cardboard. The drawback to both these materials is that after a very short time the surface will be covered in cut marks and there will be a tendency for the blade of the knife to follow a previous cut, rather than the line you are trying to follow. Vinyl floor tiles work well but tend to be a bit on the small side and they tend not to last all that long either. The very best thing to do is to invest in a proper cutting mat; these can be bought from your marquetry supplier or craft shop. They do the job well, and seem to last forever.

STRAIGHT EDGE

For cutting straight lines a steel straight edge will be required, as a wooden one is too easy to snag with the knife. An engineer's straight edge is ideal. For parquetry you will require a selection of different-width straight edges, but these can be made up, if and when you need them.

VENEER SAW

The veneer saw is a small double-edged saw for cutting the veneer where it is to be joined in a straight line against another, as with quartered tops or in parquetry assemblies. It is of course possible to use a

Selection of marquetry tools.

Sharpening the back of a knife on an oilstone.

Using a toothing plane.

Adjusting the blade.

knife for the same purpose, but you are more likely to obtain a good result with a saw, because it always cuts square and eliminates the slightly bevelled edge associated with a knife cut due to the fibres of the wood being compressed at the point of cut. The veneer saw does not have the teeth set, so it can be used against a straight edge without fear of damaging either it or the teeth.

TOOTHING PLANE

The toothing plane is rather like the old wooden smoothing plane in appearance, but with an almost upright blade. The blade itself is serrated down the front side so that when it is sharpened it has a toothed cutting edge rather than a straight one. The plane is used on any wooden groundwork that is to have veneer laid on it and serves two purposes: first, it provides a 'key' for the glue, thus giving far better adhesion, and secondly it produces a perfectly flat surface with no hollows or high-spots. In use, the surface must be planed in all directions, lengthwise, crosswise and from corner to corner, although it is best to keep a slight angle to the grain when planing across the panel. To finish you should plane in the direction of the grain. When planing near the edge of the timber you must be careful not to tip the plane and cause a dip on the edge of the work, as this would mean that in the gluing stage, no pressure would be applied to that part of the work from the press, and firm adhesion would not be achieved. The blade is adjusted by tapping with a hammer and then securing in place by firmly tapping in the wooden wedge (*see* page 13).

CABINET SCRAPE

The cabinet scrape is used for removing the shavings of wood from the finished picture before sanding, or if you have used veneers of different thicknesses in the same picture it can be used to level the back surface of the veneers before laying. It is very important that the scrape is sharp, and that it is sharpened in the correct manner, otherwise it can either tear the grain or leave scores in the surface of the work.

To sharpen a cabinet scrape, you first need to ensure that the edges of the scrape are straight, and this is achieved by holding the scrape in a vice and filing the long edges so that they are straight and at right-angles to the sides. It is perhaps a good idea to just file off the corners a little so that there is no risk of their digging into the work when in use. Now you have to hone the edges of the scrape so that you have four sharp cutting edges, and this is done by sharpening them on your oilstone, first the edge of your scrape and then the sides. The last step in the sharpening process is to turn over the newly sharpened edges with a steel or knife sharpener, in effect creating a sharp burr on each side. This is accomplished by running the steel along the edge of the scrape a few times, at first keeping it at 90 degrees to the sides, but then gradually lowering the handle to turn the burr over.

The full sharpening process just described, does not have to be followed completely each time; the first time that the edges become dull, it will be sufficient to simply place the scrape on its side near the edge of the bench, apply a little oil for lubrication, and turn the burrs back by running the steel flat along the edges. When this has been done the edges are once again turned over to form the burr. This shorter process, without the filing and honing, may be carried out once or twice between full sharpening.

To use, the scrape is held in both hands with the fingers curled around the sides and the thumbs in the middle at the back, slightly bending the scrape, which is then pushed over the surface of the work whilst

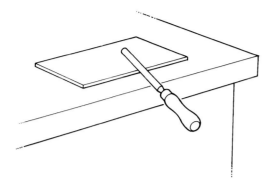

Place scrape flat on its side and remove old burr with steel knife sharpener.

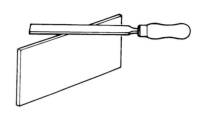

File to obtain straight edge.

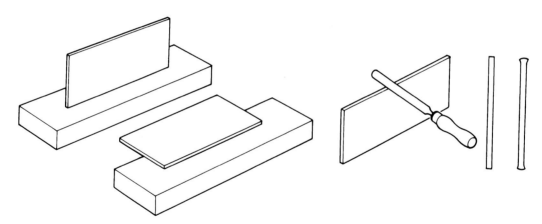

Hone edges on oil stone to obtain four sharp edges.

Turn sharpened end over with steel.

Fig 2 Sharpening a cabinet scrape.

being held at a slight angle; in this way it should be possible to remove a very fine shaving of wood. Generally the scrape is used at a slight angle to the direction of the grain of the wood.

ROLLER

An edge-roller can be used over the jointed veneers to ensure that they are a snug fit and lying flat.

A square marquetry piano in satinwood and mahogany made around 1785.

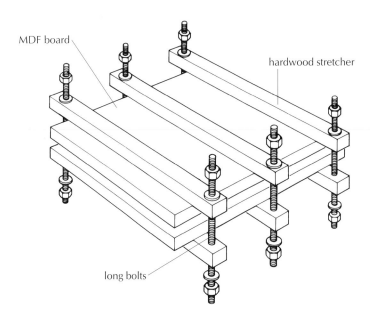

Fig 3 A veneer press or caul.

PRESS

A press or caul will be needed to hold the marquetry in place on the base board whilst the glue is drying. A cast-iron bookbinder's press is useful for small panels, if you can get hold of one; failing that you can make up your own.

You can make your press out of any two totally flat surfaces that can be cramped together without distorting. By far the best material to use is two pieces of thick MDF board with hardwood cross-stretchers. This can either be cramped together with six G-cramps, or if you prefer, the hardwood stretchers can be made so that they overhang the MDF board on each side and have holes drilled in them so that they can be pulled together with bolts, as shown. It is important that the pressure is applied from the centre first, so that excess glue is squeezed out and not trapped. For this reason the cross-stretchers are made slightly convex. If the cross-stretchers are straight, then when they are cramped down, either with G-cramps or bolts, the pressure will be applied to the outside edges first and the pressure at the centre will always be less, possibly causing the stretchers to become concave at the centre; indeed it is even possible in those circumstances that the more pressure is applied to the outside edges, the less there will be at the centre. The effect of this can be twofold: first, there may be insufficient pressure at the centre to guarantee firm contact of the veneers and ground, or there may be a build-up of glue at the centre, resulting in an uneven surface.

These problems are overcome by making the cross-stretchers slightly convex to start with. In this way the pressure is both greater and applied first at the centre and this should ensure that excess glue is squeezed out towards the edges. No matter how firmly the cramps are tightened, there should be a constant pressure across the work.

The correct way of making the cross-stretchers is to place a block of wood between and in the centre of the two stretchers to be shaped, then apply the cramps or bolts, tightening them so that the stretchers are slightly concave. While they are in this position, mark a line along the side with a straight edge, then, when the cramps or bolts are released, remove the excess wood with a spokeshave or smoothing plane. You will, in this way, end up with cross stretchers that are convex when not under pressure and that when put under pressure each side of the caul, will be perfectly flat and should exert even pressure across the work when the bolts or cramps are tightened – the pressure beginning at the centre and working towards the edge.

ADHESIVES
HOT GLUE

This of course was the only glue available to the marquetry-makers of old and required a great deal of skill and experience to be used successfully. The glue was applied to the groundwork and then allowed to cool before the surfaces were brought into contact with one another. The veneers were carefully laid in place on the groundwork and held in place with veneer pins. The press or caul was then heated, so that when the pressure was applied, the marquetry was held firmly in place as the heated caul melted the glue. The pressure was applied from the middle out, so as to expel any excess glue, and the whole thing was allowed to cool gradually.

Fortunately these days we have a variety of other glues to choose from when gluing the picture to the groundwork, but some professionals still like to use hot glue for assembling the various pieces of veneer onto paper, prior to laying.

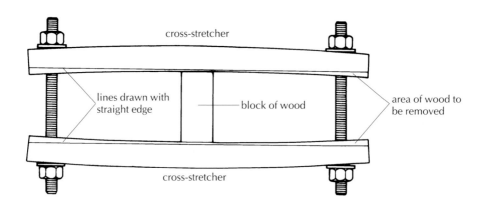

End view of press

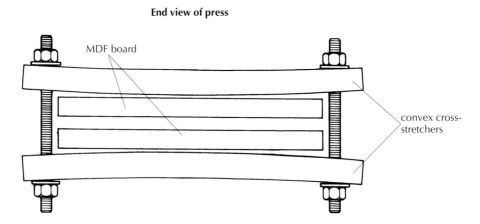

Fig 4 Making the cross-stretchers.

CASCAMITE (UREA-FORMALDEHYDE)

Cascamite is a cold-water glue that is very strong and water-resistant when dry. It is purchased as a white powder and is made up by adding the powder to cold water until you have a creamy paste. When dry, cascamite is white in appearance and will not take stain, which can result in a white line around each of the different pieces of veneer if there is a gap. This problem, however, is easily overcome by adding a small quantity of dry earth colouring pigment to the glue as soon as you have made it up. Pigments are available from any good polishing supplier and will not affect the strength of the glue. When colouring, however, you must remember that the colour of the glue when dry will be lighter than when it is wet. Cascamite needs to be held in cramps or a press until fully dry. Drying times will be given on the tin.

PVA GLUE (POLYVINYL ACETATE)

PVA, I find, is the best and easiest glue to use for marquetry. It comes ready to use, it dries almost colourless and can be used for both gluing down the final panel and for rubbing into joints when the picture has been assembled. PVA needs to be held in cramps or a press until fully dry. One important tip is to wait a few minutes before applying the glue to the veneer to allow excess water to evaporate off; in this way the veneer will have less of a tendency to curl up when it comes into contact with the glue. The best way to achieve this is to squeeze a little glue into a shallow container to allow the water to evaporate off, and then apply the glue from there.

SIZE

Some surfaces may be very porous and absorb a great deal of the glue when it is applied, possibly leaving insufficient glue for good adhesion; this is often true of chipboard. Under these circumstances it will be necessary to size the surface with a coat of diluted glue and allow it to dry before lightly sanding down and then using the glue in the normal way.

CONTACT ADHESIVE

Many people start off using contact adhesive, and will use nothing else as it has the advantage of not needing cramps. The glue has to be spread on to both surfaces to be joined, with a toothed spreader, and allowed to become touch-dry. The manufacturer's instructions will tell you how long to wait before bringing the glued surfaces together. Be sure that you have positioned everything accurately before allowing the surfaces to touch, as they will bond instantly.

The disadvantages of contact adhesives are twofold. First, it is possible for them to be adversely affected by some stains and finishes, and this could in some circumstances cause the veneer to bubble, and secondly they are quite thick – I can always recall Carlo, my friend and mentor, telling me that there were two kinds of people in the world: there are those who use glue for holding wood together; and there are those who use glue for holding wood apart. If you really get on with contact adhesive, by all means use it, especially in those circumstances where you are dealing with a very large panel and do not want to use a press, but remember Carlo's warning and don't be one of those who use it to hold wood apart.

GLUE FILM

This is purchased in a roll like greaseproof paper. It is laid on to the groundwork and heated with a domestic iron set to 'silk'. Once the glue film has cooled, the backing paper is peeled off and the veneer laid on. Heat is once again applied with the iron through the veneer to remelt the glue. Some people do lay marquetry successfully using glue film, but the need to apply heat makes the task very difficult. My advice if you want to use this method would be to lay the glue film onto the groundwork as just described, but when it comes to applying the veneer, treat it exactly like hot glue and put it into a heated caul, so that the marquetry is held firmly in place as the heat from the caul melts the glue.

VENEERS

Until the end of the eighteenth century all veneers had to be cut by sawing, at first by hand, with two workers holding a saw and cutting a log that was held vertically in a large vice. These specialist sawyers would travel between workshops, cutting the veneers from the solid timber to the requirements of the marquetry-cutter. They would modify their tools to take as little waste as possible, but even so it would not have been possible to cut many veneers per inch of timber, and those veneers must have had irregularities of thickness over their length. Later as the Industrial Revolution took hold, large circular saws powered by water or steam were used, and although there would still have been large amounts of waste, the veneers could be cut finer and of a more even thickness.

Today, although some veneer is still saw-cut, the vast majority is now cut by knife, which produces next to no waste, an even thickness throughout its length and a veneer that is fine enough to be easily cut with a craft knife.

METHODS OF CUTTING VENEER

There are different methods of cutting veneer to obtain the best result from each log, and these are as follows.

Rotary Cutting

After the log has been checked for any impurities that may be present, such as a

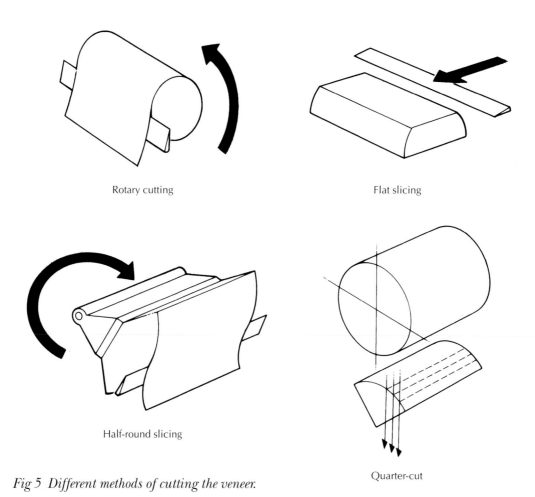

Rotary cutting

Flat slicing

Half-round slicing

Quarter-cut

Fig 5 Different methods of cutting the veneer.

stone or piece of metal that may have got into the tree as it grew or when it was felled, the tree is cut into logs of usable length and the logs are soaked in water to soften them.

The log is then mounted on a huge lathe and a knife is held against it as the lathe is rotated. The veneer is peeled away as if one was unrolling a giant Swiss roll. Veneer used for constructional purposes is cut this way, along with some decorative veneers such as bird's eye maple. As these veneers are not sequentially cut, they cannot be used to make decorative matches such as would be required for a quartered top.

Flat Slicing

The log is mounted on a flat bed and the veneers are cut straight across by the knife with the log being moved up toward the knife a veneer thickness at a time. Burr veneers are flat sliced.

Half-round Slicing

In half-round slicing the log is again fitted to a large lathe, but this time it is set off-centre so that veneer is taken from only one side of the log as it passes the knife, in this way a much wider veneer is obtained.

Quarter-cut

Some quarter-cut veneer is obtained from the centre of the log each side of the heartwood when the log is flat-sliced. However, to obtain quartered veneers from the whole log, the log is first cut in half down its length and then into quarters, these quarter-sections are then cut as near parallel to the radius of the log as possible.

Because the logs have been steamed or soaked prior to cutting, it is necessary to dry them afterwards. This can be done either by simply stacking and allowing them to dry naturally, or by kiln-drying. After drying, the veneers sometimes have their edges trimmed, and are then sorted into 'flitches' for sale – that is to say that they are arranged into batches in the same order that they were cut and tied together with string.

TYPES OF VENEER

Quarter-cut

Basically these are veneers that are cut parallel to the radius of the log.

Crown-cut

These are obtained by flat-slicing the log; however those either side of the heartwood will be quartered.

Curl Veneers

These are cut at the junction of a main branch of the tree and the trunk.

Butts

These are similar to curl but are cut from the stump of the tree where the trunk spreads towards the roots.

Burr Veneers

These are irregular sheets of veneer obtained from the protuberances on the trunks of some trees and consist of a mass of embryonic buds.

GRAIN

Straight grain Parallel to the trunk of the tree.
Irregular grain This occurs near knots.
Spiral grain The grain follows a spiral curve.
Interlocked grain Successive growth layers have produced grain in opposite directions.
Wavy grain Where the grain direction changes in waves.

GLOSSARY OF VENEERS

Afara Golden yellow, straight-grained with light mottle figure.

Afrormosia Golden brown, with a broken striped figure.

Agba Pale brown.

Ash Cream in colour with pale-brown grain.

Aspen Cream to yellow, sometimes with pinkish streaks.

Australian silky oak Red-brown with prominent medullary ray figure.

Avodire Golden yellow with a fine mottle. A good veneer for sky effects.

Ayan Yellow with mottle figure.

Beech Cream with flecked lace figure. Can be pinkish in colour if steamed.

Birch Cream with a silk-like appearance.

Birch (masur) Rotary-cut birch with a wild burr-like figure caused by beetle attack on the tree.

Birds-eye maple Cream in colour with lots of small knots or 'eyes'.

Boxwood Close-grained hard timber often used for stringing.

Bubinga Light red with a darker, fine red stripe.

Castello Yellow background with olive green swirls. Often used for water effects.

Cedar of Lebanon Creamy brown with a striped figure.

Cherry Pale creamy brown with an orange or pink stripe.

Chestnut (Horse) Very little figure, used mostly as a white wood.

Chestnut (Sweet) Similar to oak but without the ray figure.

Ebony (Macassar) Brown with beige streaks. Not to be confused with gaboon ebony, which is jet black.

Elm Light brown with darker streaks in a swirling figure.

Eucalyptus Light brown or tan with a slight mottle.

Imboia Olive brown with a wild burr lick figure.

Iroko Deep yellow with a mottled figure.

Kingwood Violet brown colour, shading almost to black.

Koto Light biscuit colour with fine grain.

Lacewood Pink with lace-like rays.

Larch Orange-brown.

Laurel Dark brown with little figure. DANGER! Laurel splinters are poisonous.

Lime Cream to white, with very little figure.

Magnolia Pale biscuit with a green tinge.

Mahogany (Honduras) Mid-brown to orange-red

Makore Cherry red with a black mottle figure.

Mansonia Light fawn to purple brown.

Maple Cream in colour.

Oak (American) Straw colour, with ray figure.

Oak (English) Brown in colour, can show ray figure.

Obeche Yellow with a ribbon stripe.

Olive ash Cream with a brown stripe.

Opepe Orange to golden-brown.

Padauk Blood red, very heavy in the solid.

Paldoa Light tan with brown stripes, has a lustrous sheen and a light mottle.

Pau rosa Reddish-brown to purple with a stripy grain.

Peartree Soft pink with very little grain.

Peroba Golden veneer with stripes.

Plaintree Pinkish brown with small fleck.

Pommelle Reddish-brown with a mottled figure. One variant with small dark areas is called 'plum pudding'.

Primavera Straw-coloured with irregular figure, often used for sky effects.

Purpleheart Purple in colour, with little figure.

Rosewood (Brazilian) Reddish-brown with darker stripes.

Rosewood (Indian) Purple, straight grain with darker stripes.

Rosewood (San Domingan) Light sand colour to reddish brown.

Rosewood (Santos) Orange brown with deep-brown figure.

Sapele Reddish-brown striped veneer.

Satinwood Golden colour with a lustrous mottled figure.

Sycamore Cream to white with lace or fiddle-back markings.

Teak Brownish straight grain with darker stripes.

Tola Reddish-brown with darker stripe.

Tropical olive Buff-coloured with irregular brown and black streaks.

Tulip Yellow background with pink and red stripes.

Walnut (African) Golden brown with striped figure.

Walnut (American) Dark brown with deep greyish-black markings.

Walnut (Australian) Brown with pinkish streaks.

Walnut (English) Grey-brown and highly figured.

Wenge Dark brown with even darker veining.

Willow White to cream in colour with wavy mottled figure.

Yew Cream to light orange with striped grain.

Zebrano Straw coloured with brown stripes.

STORING YOUR VENEERS

Veneers should always be stored in a well-ventilated and dry place; store them flat, never rolled. It is a good idea to keep a sheet or something over them to keep the dust off, and possibly a board with a weight on to keep them flat.

PREPARING THE VENEER FOR USE

This is perhaps a good time to explain that all veneers have two sides – 'Obviously', I hear you cry, but what I mean is that they have a face, or tight, smooth side, and a tension, or loose side. Generally speaking marquetry veneers are laid loose side down. 'Looseness' or 'tightness' refers to the knife checks that are present on knife-cut veneer. If you have difficulty determining which is the face side, rub the veneer

against the side of your face and you should be able to tell the smooth face side from the more rough, loose tension side. Remember, face side up when gluing, face side down for cutting.

A lot of the veneer you will come to use, no matter how well you have kept it, will be somewhat buckled and will need flattening prior to use. Lightly dampen the back of the veneer with water, place it in a press between sheets of newspaper to absorb the moisture, and leave overnight. If several sheets are being treated in this way it will be necessary to place paper between each sheet. Sometimes, especially with burr veneers, this dampening and drying process is not enough and it is necessary to use a size on the veneer. This size is made by diluting some glue with water; it must be the same glue that you intend to use for sticking down the picture and it should be diluted nine or ten parts water to one part glue. The back or loose side of the veneer is covered with the size which is then wiped off almost at once. The veneer is placed under the press overnight and care must be taken to ensure that the veneer does not stick to the press: extra paper and some candle grease on the underside of the press should do the trick. If you do use candle grease, ensure that none of it comes into contact with the veneer, as this could affect the gluing later on.

THE DESIGN

The first thing you need if you are going to produce a marquetry picture, be it with knife or saw, is a pattern or copy of your picture on paper; in fact, for some techniques, several copies are required. It may be of interest at this point to explain how the problem of making several copies of the design was overcome in the eighteenth century.

The whole design, if it was not too large, was drawn up on a sheet of paper. In cases where the design was very large it may have been divided up into smaller units and each unit treated as a whole. Once the design was drawn up on paper it was pricked – that is to say, small holes were pricked along all the lines of the design. These holes were quite fine and were made close enough together that they made a continuous line, but far enough apart that the design stayed intact. In the eighteenth century these holes were made by a hand-held, treadle-operated device that had a long overhead arm from which the pricking needle was suspended. Today it is possible to purchase an electrically operated pricking machine, but such items would only be of use to a factory producing large quantities of marquetry. The master copy having been perforated in this manner was then placed over a sheet of plain paper and the design was then pounced with a fine bitumen powder from a pounce bag. A pounce bag was made of coarse rag tied with string, that would allow the powder inside to escape when lightly knocked and then rubbed over the perforated design, causing some of the powder to go through the fine holes onto the paper beneath. In this way the design was transferred onto the plain paper and the line of powder was then secured by heating the paper almost to scorching point. As many patterns as required could be made in this manner, and it was very accurate. These days it is easy to obtain as many copies as one wants, as long as the design is not too large, simply by getting the original photocopied; it is even possible to have the design enlarged or reduced in size in this way.

It may well be that your first attempt at marquetry will be by purchasing a kit, in which case you will be supplied with a copy of the design and all you will have to do is obtain some further copies, either by tracing them yourself or getting them photocopied. If you are going to use the window technique, then one copy of the design will

be enough, but I always feel it is a good idea to have a back-up, and if you are going to work from the reverse side, then you will need to have the design reversed. Later on, however, you will want to make your own design from a photograph or print, or even to make your own original drawing. If this is the case, and you are going to use a print, then you first have to consider whether the photograph or print is suitable for a marquetry picture – remember that every line and change of colour or contrast on the original will have to be a joint between veneers in your marquetry picture. Study the picture carefully – it may be that although the original picture is very complicated, it will lend itself to being simplified. Perhaps all the intricate details need not be shown, many details in the background could be simplified, or left out entirely. It is possible that some areas that would at first appear to need several veneers, can in fact be represented by one carefully chosen veneer with the right grain, or perhaps just one section of detail from the original can be picked out to make a pleasing subject on its own. The secret is to be flexible in your approach to the problems.

When you have decided on a picture, you will need to make a copy or tracing of it. Place the picture on a flat surface with a sheet of tracing paper over the face. If it is possible to hinge the tracing paper with masking tape along the top edge without risking damage to the print when the tape is peeled off, this is an advantage, because it enables you to lift the tracing paper in order to check details underneath and lay it flat again in exactly the same place. It will be necessary to remove the print from any frame it may be in at the time. Trace over the picture underneath, in as much detail as you want to appear in your marquetry; do not draw in any details that are not going to feature in the end result. If any of the details you want to appear are not very visible through the tracing paper, they can be drawn in after. Alternatively, if the whole picture is quite dark and difficult to see through the tracing paper, you can place a piece of plain white paper underneath the picture. Hinge this along the top edge and slip a piece of carbon paper between the two, carbon side to the white paper. Now go over the picture with a stylus of some kind, possible a fine knitting needle, taking care not to damage the original picture and lifting the picture and carbon paper occasionally to check that the image is being transferred to the plain sheet. If it is not possible to trace the original picture without causing some damage to it then I would suggest that you take a photograph of the painting, as this opens up other possibilities. It is possible these days to have a photocopy made of a photograph, and this will allow you to have it enlarged or reduced in size. Alternatively you can use a pantograph to make you own enlargement of the photograph. Another alternative is to take a colour transparency of the original and project it onto a piece of white paper that has been taped to the back of a door or other flat surface, and simply trace around it. Using transparencies has another advantage. If you have a picture of, let's say a steam train in the country, but the picture was taken from a distance and the train is too small, you can adapt your picture by projecting it onto the paper and tracing in the background, but then move the projector further away to project the train, thus making it larger. In this way you can also incorporate bits from other slides – the possibilities are endless.

In most cases when you are cutting a marquetry picture, it is best to work from the back of the veneers, that is to say that the picture or design you are working from should be reversed. The reason for this is

Support your arm while cutting.

explained below. The easiest way to reverse your drawing is to place a sheet of carbon paper underneath, carbon side to the back of your drawing, and trace over the design. The design will be reproduced on the back of the paper. Alternatively you could place another sheet of plain paper between the picture and the carbon paper. In this way you will obtain a reversed drawing on a new sheet of paper.

KNIFE-CUTTING TECHNIQUE

The first and most important thing to remember is that it is absolutely essential to have a sharp knife – this point cannot be stressed too much: it will not be possible to obtain a good result if the knife you are using has a dull edge. A good oilstone should always be on hand, along with a piece of rag to keep both stone and blade clean. It is important not to get any oil onto the veneer as this will have an adverse effect on the gluing process, remember to keep all things as clean as possible at all times.

Mostly, a couple of wipes over the oilstone at regular intervals will keep the point of the blade sharp. There are two ways that this can be done, either by honing the bevel of the knife in the conventional way or by rubbing away the back of the blade so that a new and unused section of the blade comes into use. Some people will sharpen the back edge of the blade to a double bevel as well, making the blade diamond-shape in section rather than triangular, as they feel this is less likely to compress the veneer at the point of cut, making for an easier cut. Whether or not you sharpen your blade in this manner is something you will decide in time. When cutting the veneer it is important to be comfortable and for the hand to be supported. Unless you are cutting against a straight edge you will not be able

to follow a line if your hand holding the knife is hanging in mid air, so rest your arm and wrist on the cutting mat for support. Try to position the veneer so that you are cutting towards yourself and are able to see clearly the line you are cutting. As you progress through the cut, turn the veneer so that you are always cutting toward yourself; do not be tempted to turn your wrist. Sometimes, if you would prefer not to keep moving the veneer, it might be practical to cut standing up, so that you can slowly work your way around the table you are working on, but generally it will be more comfortable to be seated.

If the line you are following requires a long, sweeping cut, you will be able to keep the handle of the knife raised about 50 degrees from the table, but as the curve you are cutting gets sharper, the handle of the knife will have to be raised higher: generally speaking, the longer the cut the lower the handle, the sharper the curve the higher the handle. The cutting motion itself needs to be fairly short and controlled. Do not be tempted to use too much pressure, pushing hard with the knife only makes it more difficult to stay on line, and it is more likely that you will break the blade, which is both infuriating and expensive. It is not necessary to cut right through the veneer in one go – far better to make several light passes, and if one part has not quite separated, cut again – don't be tempted to break it away with your fingers. If the shape you are cutting has any delicate corners or fine protuberances, make sure you cut away from these, rather than towards them; remember it is always possible to stick a little Sellotape on to these areas to protect them during cutting and to ensure that no little ends get lost.

It has already been said that the longer the cut, the lower the handle of the knife should be held. If one is cutting a sharp curve or a wavy line it will probably be best to do this in a 'step cut'. This is a series of

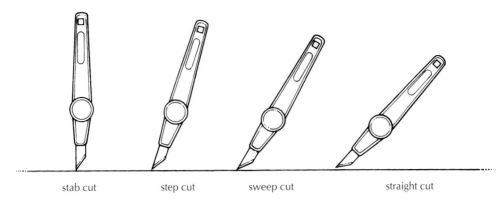

stab cut   step cut   sweep cut   straight cut

Fig 6 The sharper the curve, the higher the handle.

short cuts with a small gap between each one. This should make it easier to follow the contours of the design. You can then go over the line again in the same way, but this time starting the cuts from the middle of the first ones, gradually joining the cuts together and continuing in this way until the veneer is released.

If the curve is too much even for a step cut, or if you are dealing with a jagged edge, you can use a stabbing or pricking action, with the knife almost upright. These stab cuts are joined together in a series the same as the step cuts. It is good practice when cutting something jagged to cover the area with Sellotape to prevent areas of short grain breaking away. Remember, too, that when cutting out a jagged area – a Christmas tree for example – you do not have to cut out the window intact, it may be a good idea to cut out the centre of the window as a rectangle or oval at first, and then cut into the jagged areas. First cut out the bulk of the centre as one large chunk. This way, you should find it easier to cut out the complicated edge in step or stab cuts by returning to the centre each time; remember to tape any vulnerable edges. Likewise with the insert, it will be easier to cut the required piece out of a small section of veneer, so that you can run your cuts to the outer edge of the veneer piece each time, rather than from a large piece that you want to keep intact for later use. Again, remember to cut away from and to tape vulnerable edges. Don't forget that it is possible to obtain some blades that have a bevel only on one side – you may like to see how you get on with one of these.

Always remember it is far better to use a lot of gentle cuts rather than one or two forceful ones. If the knife blade shows a tendency to jam in the veneer it may be that you are using to much pressure; if not, you can wipe the blade on a candle and this should lubricate it. Be careful with the candle grease, though, as it may make it more difficult to glue the pattern together when assembling the marquetry, if there is any grease on the edges of the veneer.

Now there is another decision to be made. Do we work face side up or face side down? There are two schools of thought on that. If we work on the reverse side, i.e. the side face up on the bench when we are working is the side that will eventually be glued down onto the groundwork, then the joint will be a tighter fit on the face side, the side face down on the bench, than on the reverse. This is because the knife will inevitably compress the fibres of the veneer and produce a vee-shaped cut, a

Fig 7 (a) Cut out the centre of the window first.

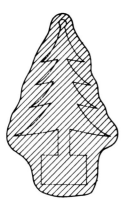

(b) Reduce the area of veneer before cutting the shape.

good close fit underneath but slightly open on top. This would suggest that working from the reverse side is the best, and most manuals on marquetry will tell you to do things this way, and many marquetarians stand by this, but we have to remember that the picture has to be sanded and cleaned up ready for finishing. If we have worked from the face, then the gap between the veneers should get smaller as the picture is sanded and cleaned up, however if we have worked from the reverse and have good close joints, these joints will inevitably become more open as we sand them down. On balance, I feel I must agree that the experienced marquetarian will do better working from the reverse, with a reversed drawing, but I do not want to give the impression that it is a hard and fast rule, and if you feel that you may have to do a lot of cleaning up when your picture is complete, or if you just think you will be happier working from the front, for whatever reason, then please feel free to do so. You will inevitably develop your own preferences as you progress with you marquetry.

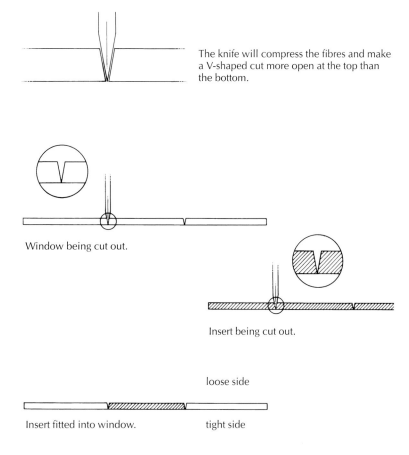

Fig 8 Face and reverse sides.

The knife will compress the fibres and make a V-shaped cut more open at the top than the bottom.

Window being cut out.

Insert being cut out.

loose side

Insert fitted into window.   tight side

It can be seen that if the loose side is sanded down to prepare for polishing the gaps will get smaller, whereas if the tight side is sanded the gaps will get bigger.

THE WINDOW METHOD

The window method of marquetry is one of the best and easiest way of producing good quality knife-cut marquetry pictures. It is accurate, and it allows scope for slightly altering the design as you work, should this be necessary, either to improve the line or to hide a bad cut, particularly in an early attempt at marquetry. The window method also enables you to see the effect of the grain direction on the design and alter it before cutting; it puts you in the enviable position of being able to see what things will actually look like before you cut out the wood.

The first step is to obtain a piece of plain easy to cut veneer such as sycamore to act as a waster. It is possible to use cardboard for this purpose, which is probably a good idea if you are working on a design that has a complicated background. But if, for example, the background you are working with is just sea and sky, it will save you some cutting if you join these two together in the appropriate place and use them as your waster. It is in these veneers that the first 'windows' will be cut, and they need to be slightly larger than the overall dimension of your design. The next step is to fix on top of the waster the piece of paper on which the design is drawn. The paper must be hinged with masking tape or Sellotape tape along the top edge of the waster, so that it can be lifted and set down again in exactly the same place on the veneer each time. It is a good idea to make a small check mark on the bottom edge of the paper, corresponding to a mark on the bottom of the waster, as a double check to make sure the design is returned to the exact position each time. An alternative to placing check marks is to have the design photocopied on to transparent sheet. In this way you have a visual check each time, and you can see the picture at all times.

Now it is time to decide which will be the first window to cut out. Always select a part of the design that is in the background. If you are making a landscape picture, for instance, the sky would be the obvious first piece to cut into your waster, unless of course you have decided to use the sky veneer itself as your waster and to save some cutting, in which case, distant mountains or fields might be chosen. Start with the larger areas of background, ignoring smaller details and foreground objects. The reason for this is to save the continuity of grain on items that might be split or separated by other objects. Imagine, for

instance, that there was a lake in your picture, and that a tree, telegraph pole or some other object split the image of it in two. If you were to cut the tree first, it would be difficult to cut in the lake afterwards in two sections either side and keep the grain constant across the picture – even a small deviation would be strikingly obvious. By cutting the lake first, you ensure that the grain is continuous, and you can split it with the tree later without worry.

In the beginner's example I have used a cat, which was purchased as a kit. (Sorry about the bad joke, cat lovers! I know most cats are purchased as kits.) The first window to be cut out is the main body, ignoring the bow tie and the claws for the time being, as these will be cut in later. Place a piece of carbon paper between the paper design, or transparent sheet as used here, and the waster, carbon side to the veneer, and trace over the first window to be cut, so that its outline is transferred onto the waster. Turn back the design and transfer the waster to the cutting mat. Carefully cut out the first window, remembering to keep the knife almost upright, and always to cut towards yourself. Do not use too much pressure and risk breaking the blade, the first cut is just a scoring cut to mark the outline of the window, and to provide a tramline for the knife to follow in subsequent cuts. Make several small cuts around the

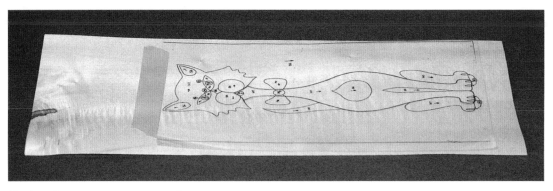

Design drawn on transparent sheet.

Harry.

window, and make sure that the window is cut right through all the way round before trying to remove it. If you are not sure whether it is cut all the way through there are two ways to tell. Either you can try stabbing the veneer with your knife to see if it will lift out clean, as it should do if your cutting is successfully, or you can lift up the waster itself and hold it against the light to see if the cut is visible all the way round from the back. If it is not, return to the mat and continue cutting.

Once the window has been cut out, place the chosen veneer for the body underneath the waster and view it through the 'window'. You can move it around to select the best area and direction of grain – this is one of the advantages of the window method. When you are sure you have the veneer in the best position, carefully turn the veneer and the waster over and tape the veneer in place to prevent it moving during cutting. Turn the veneers back over and make a score-cut around the edge of the window to mark the veneer underneath. Do not try to cut it out yet: this first cut is simply to mark the outline and provide a tramline for the knife to follow. If you are using a knife that has a bevel on both sides, it will be necessary to angle the blade slightly to ensure that the cut is tight up against the edge of the window. It is possible to obtain a knife that has a bevel on one side only, and these are very useful for this purpose and for cutting against a straightedge. Remove the object veneer from under the waster and place it on the cutting mat. Examine the piece you are about to cut, to determine whether there are any vulnerable areas of short grain that might break away when being cut. If there are, then these areas should have some Sellotape stuck over them to prevent bits being lost; remember always to cut away from these areas. Sometimes the score line will be difficult to see, if this is the case, you can either use a very finely sharpened pencil that will easily follow the line and mark it before you commence to cut, or you can rub a little whiting into the score cut to show it up. Whiting is fine white powder, very like talc in appearance, that can be obtained from any art shop, although they may know it as gesso powder. Whiting mixed with hot glue size makes gesso, which is the basis of many a gilt mirror and is the substance that artists use to fill woodgrain before applying paint.

Decide what type of cut will be necessary: can you make a continuous cut, or will

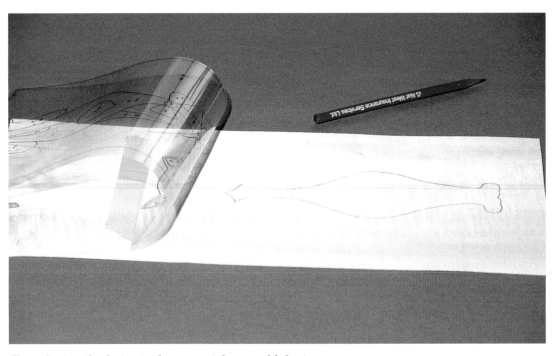

Transferring the design to the veneer (above and below).

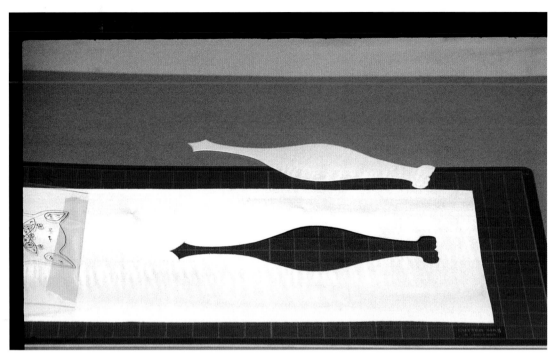

The first window is cut out.

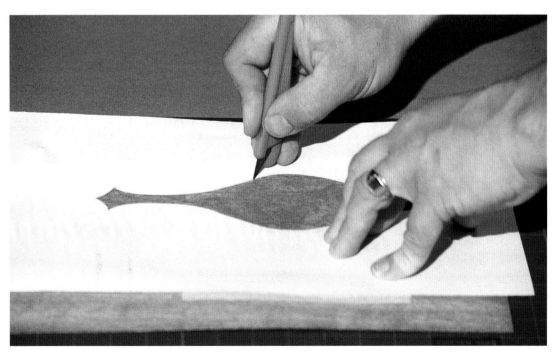

Score-cutting the first insert.

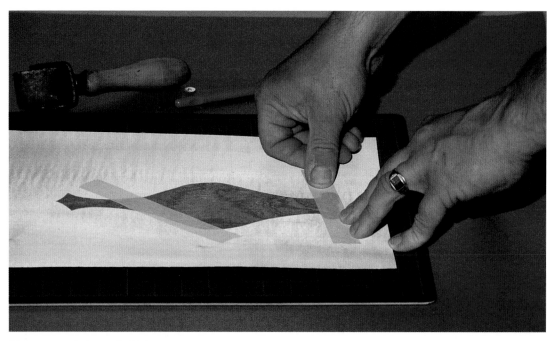

Veneer tape helps to hold larger pieces.

The second window.

it have to be a step or a stab cut? With the veneer on the cutting mat, carefully cut out the object following the score cut you made when the veneer was under the waster. Have the waster on the surface you are going to use for assembling the picture; this should be a perfectly flat surface such as a work top, which is easily kept clean. Fit the piece you have just cut out, into the window in the waster, hopefully it will be a tight fit and will need to be coaxed into position. Now rub a little glue into the joint to hold it in place – PVA glue is ideal for this purpose. Wipe off any excess glue and use a roller to make sure that the veneers are flat and that you do not have one edge proud of the other. The glue is best rubbed in from the reverse side of your drawing to keep the face clean, remember that if you are working from a reversed drawing, this means that the glue is rubbed in on the side you are working from. The piece just

inserted will now have to be left for a few minutes to dry. If the piece you have just fitted is a large area, it will be a good idea to tape it in place from the underside rather than to rely on the glue alone. If the work is to be left for a period of time, it is best if it has a flat piece of wood placed on it with a weight to keep the work flat.

Having given the glue a few minutes to dry you can start cutting the second window, in this case, the cat's head. The procedure is exactly the same as for the first window: position the drawing over the waster with carbon paper between and mark onto the waster the section of the design that you are about to cut. Cut out the second window in the same way as the first, taping any vulnerable areas, and then once again place the chosen veneer underneath the window and arrange so that the most suitable area of grain shows through. The grain for the cat's body was straight vertical,

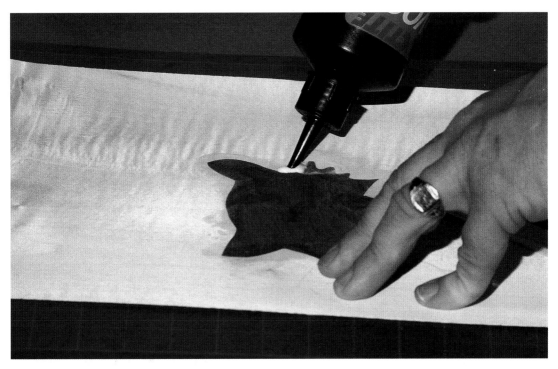

Rubbing glue into the joint.

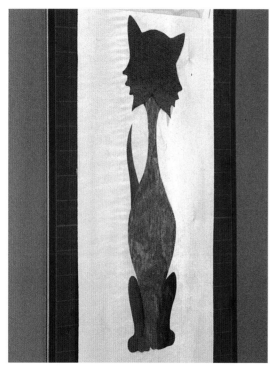

The tail in place.

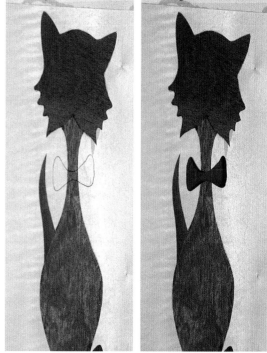

Marking and cutting the bow tie.

but for the head it is at a slight angle to give the impression that the head is tilted to the side. Tape the veneer onto the underside to prevent it from moving whilst it is being cut and score cut around the edge of the window to mark it. Transfer the veneer to the cutting mat and cut out the section of head. Insert the section of head into the second window and secure by rubbing glue into the joint as before on a flat surface. Clean and allow to dry. The next two sections to be cut can be the back legs, the two windows are cut out as before and the veneer placed under the windows. Again, the grain is arranged at an angle to that of the body, this time each leg splaying out. The tail can then be treated in the same way.

So far, each piece that we have cut has been let into the background veneer or waster only, but now the bow tie is to be cut. This will mean cutting a window that is a combination of the waster and the body of the cat. The process is exactly same as before, but care must be taken at the junction of two different types of veneer, as one may be more easily cut than the other, and this may cause the knife to go off line. Cut carefully across the junction, without too much pressure. It is also a good idea to tape the back of such junctions, or Sellotape on the top if you prefer, in case there is any short grain involved, just to make doubly certain that no small corners break off and get lost.

The next few windows, like the cat's belly, can be cut in the conventional way, but there are two ways that the eyes can be dealt with. Either they can be cut in the same as the other parts – largest piece first and ending up cutting in the pupil – or you can take a piece of the green-tinted veneer that is to represent the iris and place this on the work, then bring the design down over it with carbon paper between and mark the outline of the pupil. When I did this I had to use a stab cut to cut out the pupil window. Then I placed the veneer for the pupil under the window and cut this out, then glued it into the iris veneer. Secondly, I took the veneer that was to represent the white of the cat's eye, placed this veneer on the work so that I could mark the outline of the iris on it and cut this window out. Then I placed the iris veneer with the pupil already cut in, under this window and was able to move the veneer about until I had the pupil in exactly the place I wanted it. I carefully turned the assembly over to tape it in that position, then turned it back, cut it out and secured it in its window. All that remained to be done then was to carry out the same procedure as before with the window for the eye socket. The eye socket window was cut out and I was able to place the white of the eye veneer with the iris and pupil in place under the window

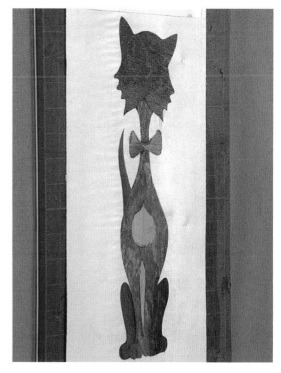

More pieces inserted.

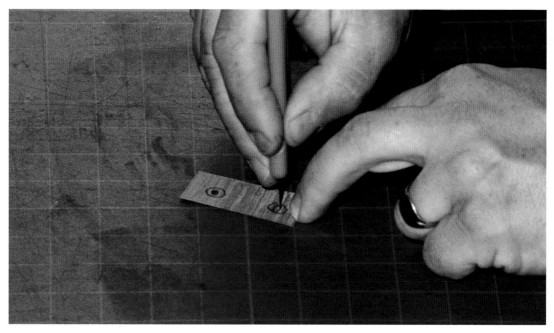

Stab cutting.

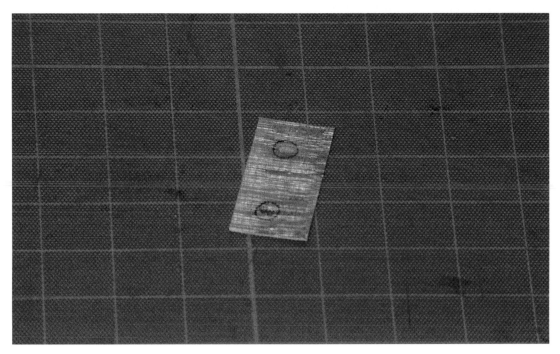

Cutting and gluing the pupil of the eye (above and below).

and arrange them in the best possible position before taping and cutting. The second eye was treated in exactly the same way and the remaining facial feature cut in.

Positioning and cutting the iris (above and below).

The Bevel Cut

We have seen how cutting the veneer with a knife makes a vee-shaped cut that has a loose side and a tight side. Many marquetarians maintain that you should always work from the reverse side so that the side that has the tight joints is the side that will eventually be the face of the picture, and that to achieve this it is necessary to work from a reversed drawing. We have seen that there are two ways to look at this problem. As you sand down from the tight side the joints will open up, and the more you sand the more open they will become. For this reason, some marquetarians will work from the face side and eliminate the need to reverse the drawing, but clearly there is a slight problem with either method. When I say there is a problem, I don't want to confuse the issue or get this all out of

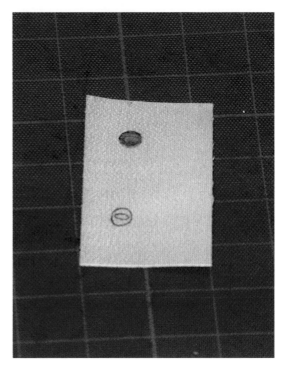

The eye.

are very small, and will most probably be filled with glue or some kind of filler in any case. Do not unduly worry yourself early on in your marquetry career – it is possible to produce very fine pictures, working from either front or reverse. It is, however, every marquetarians aim to perfect his techniques and there is a way in which the problem of being able to work from the front of the design without having to worry about tight or loose sides can be solved; this is by bevel-cutting. With bevel-cutting you will be able to obtain a close-fitting square-butted joint that should stay a constant width throughout the sanding down and cleaning up process.

to confuse the issue or get this all out of proportion: if the veneers have been cut accurately, the gaps we are talking about

The problem we wish to eliminate is that of a vee-shaped cut, caused by the bevels of the knife compressing the fibres of the

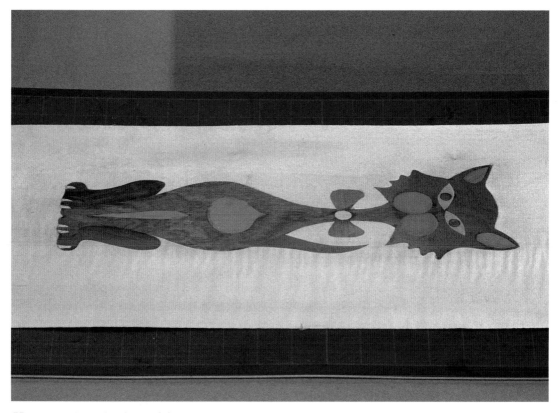

Harry awaiting border and frame.

A superb credenza. The credenza was a piece of Victorian drawing room furniture with a large centre door and bow glazed doors at either end for display, often decorated with marquetry panels and brass mounts.

veneer on each side. It is possible to obtain a square-cut edge to the window if we angle the knife inwards towards the insert when cutting, i.e. we keep one edge of the bevel of the knife upright, or at right-angles to the surface of the veneer. In this way, any compression of the veneer will take place only on the waste side, that part of the window that is to be discarded. Likewise, if we angle the blade of the knife outwards when cutting the insert we will obtain a square edge to it, the compression again only being on the waste side of the cut. Then when we position the insert into the window, we should have a close-fitting square-butted joint between the two.

Try each of these methods of cutting in turn, so that you are completely familiar with working from the reverse of the drawing, the front of the drawing and with bevel-cutting.

THE TEMPLATE METHOD

The template method of marquetry-cutting is so called because each new piece of veneer is used as a template to trim the edge of the veneers it joins that have been previously laid. The design is drawn on tracing paper and hinged to the top of the base board in the same way as for the window method, so that it can be brought down over the veneers, with carbon paper between for marking. In the example, of the remains of Wheal Coats engine-house at Chapel beach in Cornwall, the sky veneer is cut to fit the top of the base board, but some excess is left at the bottom edge where it would join the land and sea. The sky veneer is glued in place on the groundwork with a quick-drying or contact adhesive, but great care is needed to ensure that the glue only covers a little beyond the line that will eventually be cut, and that the

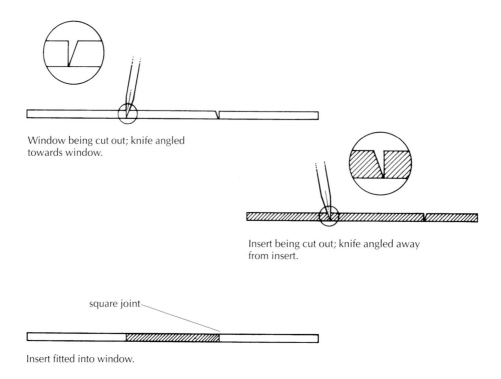

Window being cut out; knife angled towards window.

Insert being cut out; knife angled away from insert.

square joint

Insert fitted into window.

Fig 9 Angling the blade for a square cut.

base board is kept clean. Because each piece of veneer is glued in place after cutting directly to the groundwork, this method is sometimes referred to as the 'Stick as you go' method. Next the piece of veneer that will represent the far coast is placed in position under the design and marked out. It is then transferred to the cutting mat and cut out accurately only where it meets the sky veneer; in all other places it is left oversize so that it can be trimmed off later. The coast veneer just cut is then placed in its exact position on the groundwork where it will overlap the sky veneer so that it can be used as a template. The bottom of the sky veneer is carefully cut out by scribing a cut along the top edge of the coast. Now the coast veneer is removed and a cut made along the scribe line just made until the sky veneer is cut right through. The excess sky veneer is then prised

off and discarded, and any trace of glue carefully removed. The coast veneer can then be glued in place. Neither the sky nor the coast veneer are cut where the engine-house chimney dissects them so that continuity of grain is preserved, which would be difficult if the far coast was cut as two separate sections.

As far as possible it is best to work from top to bottom of your picture and from background to foreground, so the next piece of veneer to be cut will be that for the sea. Once again, continuity of grain has to be taken into account when deciding whether to cut the sea as one or two pieces of veneer and in this case it is best to cut the sea as one, because the two areas are only separated by a relatively small margin and any discrepancy in the grain on either side would be obvious. Again the sea veneer will be positioned on the board and have the outline marked on it by bringing the design down over the top with carbon paper between. It is then taken to the cutting mat where it is cut accurately along the top so that it can be used as a template for cutting the bottom of the far coast, but again extra veneer is left around the rest of the veneer, so that it can be trimmed off later. The sea veneer is positioned in place and its top edge used as a template to scribe cut the bottom edge of the far coast. Once again the coast veneer is cut through to the base board and the excess veneer prised away; any remaining glue is cleaned off. After the sea veneer is glued in place, it will be possible to cut another piece of coastline, that at the top left of the picture, to be used it as a template for cutting into both the far coast and the left side of the sea veneer. Continue cutting and gluing in this manner down the left-hand side of the chimney, leaving extra veneer to be trimmed away at the bottom each time until the chimney itself can be fitted. Once the chimney veneer is in place the area of beach to the right of the engine-house should be fitted. Now the veneers of the engine-house itself can be cut and glued, starting with the back wall. The arched door-way can be fitted and lastly the area of hilltop in the foreground. When using this method of marquetry cutting, the picture has to be studied carefully prior to cutting, in order to work out a cutting sequence, working from background to foreground. The sequence I have described here is not the only one, or even necessarily the best one that could be used. Study the picture and the sequence of cutting yourself to see if you think it should be done differently.

The fact that this method of cutting has been chosen does not mean that no other can be used in the same picture. It may be that the window in the back wall of the engine-house would be better being cut into the wall by the window method prior to the wall veneer being cut, rather than cutting it into the far wall after it has been glued in place. It is always possible to use two or more different methods of cutting in the same picture, if it would give a better result.

Because the veneers are stuck down as the work progresses in this method, a fast-acting glue or contact adhesive is required, and it will probably be a good idea to veneer the back of the ground board before work commences, in order to counteract the tendency for it to warp as glue is applied to the picture.

It is possible to work from the front of the design, as shown here, or from the back with a reverse design. When working from the back, the veneers are glued in place on a piece of stiff card or craft paper as the work progresses, and are then transferred to the groundwork on completion, when the craft paper is removed from the front of the picture.

This method of sticking as you go is very useful for applied marquetry when veneer is to be glued onto a curved surface such as a turned table lamp or trinket bowl.

The sky veneer.

The coast veneer.

The sea veneer.

More coastline.

The completed picture.

two

FRETSAWING

TOOLS

THE FRETSAW (HAND-HELD)

Fretsaws are all basically the same in design, the only difference being in weight or depth of throat. Obviously the deeper the throat on the fretsaw, the larger the panel that can be cut in one go, and this would seem to be an advantage; however, one must also consider the fact that the larger the saw the more difficult it will be to control. In practice, most fretsaws have about a 30cm throat, and this should be big enough for most purposes. Some enterprising mar-

quetarians manage to adapt their saws for larger jobs, by cutting through the frame before the U-bend and extending it by bolting on a length of metal, or, if the saw has a round section frame, by inserting a length of dowel rod. but if you have a very large panel it might be worth considering separating it into more manageable sections and gluing them together when the overall picture is laid.

The saw holds the fretsaw blades in a clamp at each end, and to fix a new blade in the saw, you should attach the blade into the clamp at the handle end first with the teeth pointing towards the handle, so that

The hand-held fretsaw.

the cut is on the down stroke of the saw. Now place the other side of the frame against the side of the bench and press so as to squeeze the two sides of the saw frame together, enough to be able to insert the other end of the blade between the clamps and tighten them. When taking the blade out you must again position it against the bench to take up the tension; never just release the clamp, as this will cause the saw to spring apart quite violently and may damage the veneer you are cutting.

For most cutting operations the saw is held vertical and the veneer held horizontally or at a slight angle on the cutting table. Some marquetarians go to great lengths to rig up apparatus that will hold the saw in the correct position and also to enable it to be operated by a foot treadle so that both hands are left free to hold and guild the veneer; this can be a cheap alternative to purchasing an electric fretsaw.

FRETSAW BLADES

There are basically four standard fretsaw blades, all 130mm in length. There is the single-tooth blade, type 570, which is suitable for general wood cutting, the double-tooth blade, type 560, for use on wood, plastic, hardboard etc. and for marquetry, special helical/spiral piercing blades, and the very fine metal-cutting blade, suitable for brass, aluminium and other alloys: Blades 570 and 560 come in sizes 3, 2, 1 and 2/0, 3 being the coarsest; Piercing blades come in sizes 1, 0 and 2/0, and Metal-cutting blades in sizes 1, 2/0, 4/0 and 6/0.

FRETSAW (TREADLE)

It is still possible to buy a treadle fretsaw, which will have a much deeper throat than that of the hand-held type. Once you get used to operating the treadle and keeping a more or less constant speed going, the treadle fretsaw offers the advantage of leaving both hands free to guide the work; it also helps to keep you fit!

FRETSAW (ELECTRIC)

The obvious advantages of an electric fretsaw are that you have both hands free for guiding the work, the speed is constant and you do not have to operate a treadle. The disadvantage is that they tend to be quite expensive.

CUTTING TABLE OR BIRD'S MOUTH

This is the table or platform on which the veneers are held whilst being cut. The table needs to be both rigid and large enough to support a reasonable-sized piece of veneer.

Treadle fretsaw.

47

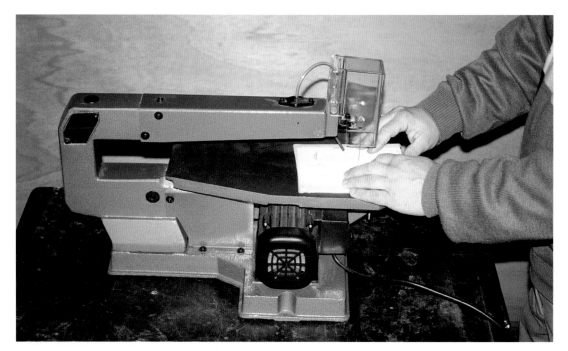

Electric fretsaw.

The bird's mouth.

Many Dutch craftsmen came to England during the reign of William and Mary and their influence can be seen in the furniture of the time, as with this beautiful chest of drawers.

Most are made so that they can be held in a vice, although there is no reason why you cannot have one that is a permanent fixture somewhere. The cutting table is sometimes referred to as a bird's mouth because of the shape of the vee-cut that is made in it, having a small hole through which the fretsaw blade passes and a vee-shaped cut to give easy access. Some more elaborate tables are made so that they can be tilted in order that the work can be cut at an angle whilst keeping the saw itself upright. In practice, however, if you require a tilted table, most of them can simply be put into the vice at the desired angle. The tilting table is necessary for more advanced fretsaw cutting.

DONKEY

The donkey (*see* Fig 1) is a device used by marquetry-cutters of old and also by some professional cutters today, consisting of a bench on which the cutter sits with the fretsaw supported to the side, almost at eye-level. The work is held upright before the cutter in a vice that can be opened and closed quickly by means of a foot pedal. In this way the cutter uses one hand to operate the fretsaw and the other to move and rotate the work in the vice. Producing marquetry panels while moving the work with one hand, operating the saw with the other and using a foot to operate the vice requires a great deal of dexterity and practice.

PRICKER

A pricker is anything that is capable of making a hole in the veneers through which the fretsaw blade can be passed – a needle mounted in some kind of handle or a bradawl that has been ground or filed down in size. Either will do the trick; the hole itself must be made where two or more of the design lines meet.

ARCHIMEDEAN SCREW DRILL

This is a small drill that is operated by holding the top steady while pushing a collar up and down the length of the threaded drill shank. It is used as an alternative to the pricker when the sandwich of veneers is quite thick.

FRETSAW CUTTING TECHNIQUE

INTRODUCTION: YOU DON'T HAVE TO STICK TO ONE METHOD

When cutting a marquetry picture of some complexity, it is not necessary to use only one of the methods of cutting we discuss here – it may be that one part of the picture would be better cut by a different method from another. For example, you may feel it would be quicker to cut out the bulk of the picture by the patch method, but that some of the elements or details in the picture would benefit from the fretsaw window method; or you may feel more comfortable cutting a certain part with a knife – the choice is yours. Always remember to be flexible and innovative in your approach.

THE FLAT BED

Whenever you are cutting veneer with a saw, be it hand-held or electric, you will need to have a piece of waste veneer underneath the one you require in order to give support to the veneer and to take the 'rag' of the saw. You can purchase construction veneers that are much thicker than the normal veneer, and these make an excellent bottom layer for sawing. The design that you are cutting should be pasted onto the top veneer; this also helps to keep the veneer intact and stops small sections of end-grain from becoming detached and lost. This means that even when you only want to cut a single veneer, you will in fact make up a sandwich consisting of a bottom waster veneer for support, the veneer that you actually require and the top layer of paper with the design on it. In most cases when using a flat table there will be at least two layers, sometimes more.

The layers of the 'sandwich' or 'packet' have to be held together in some way to prevent them from separating as the blade moves through them, or from moving in respect to one another whilst being cut, and this can be achieved by making all the veneers in the packet the same size and shape and then taping the edges together with masking tape. If the packet of veneers is fairly large in overall size it is also a good idea to apply a few spots of glue such as cow gum or Copydex, which is easily removed when dry, between layers. Alternatively the veneers can be stapled together or pinned with veneer pins through parts of the veneers that will be discarded. The main problem, once the veneers have been cut, is in separating the layers; that is why it is important to use a glue that can be easily separated after drying.

The glue should not be used to cover the whole surface of the veneer as this would make separation very difficult – only a few small areas should be glued, just enough to keep the layers together and prevent them being pulled apart by the action of the saw blade. Veneers glued with this adhesive can be separated by inserting a table knife between the layers and carefully slicing

A sandwich of veneers for fretsawing (above and below).

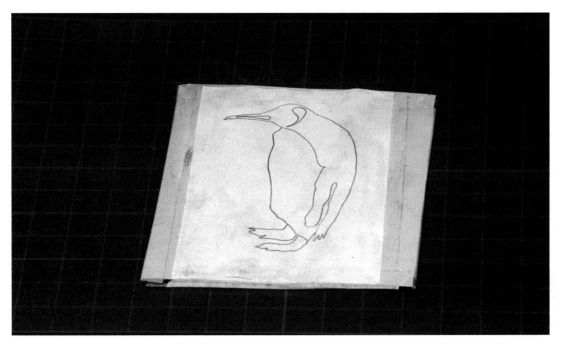

The design is pasted to the top.

Veneers interchanged after cutting.

them apart; the glue itself is easily removed by rubbing with the fingers. If the sandwich of veneers is quite small in area, it may be sufficient to hold the edges of the sandwich together with masking tape only, or the packet of veneers can be cramped together with a block of wood each side and glue applied to the edges of the packet. The cramp and wooden blocks are removed just prior to cutting when the glue is fully dry.

The simplest type of pattern to start off with is made by using just two contrasting veneers – sycamore and a dyed black, for example. These two veneers are put together in a sandwich as just described, a waster veneer on the bottom and the two veneers required and then the design is pasted onto the top veneer. The pricker is used to make a small hole through the veneers, so that the fretsaw blade can be inserted. Make as few holes as possible and try to put them at a junction where lines of your design meet, rather than half-way along a line, as the holes will be less obvious when the work is complete. If there are any 'island' areas, completely inside another, then you will of course have to make a separate hole for these, rather than cut across to them through a section of picture. Make sure that the blade is inserted into the saw and through the sandwich of veneers, so that it cuts on the downward stroke; remember the teeth are very small and it is not difficult to insert the blade upside down. If your eyes aren't as good as they once were, you can always run a finger gently down the blade – it should feel smooth on the way towards the handle and rough going away from it.

Now that you have the blade inserted in the veneers, they must be held down firmly on the sawing table as close to the blade as possible, being very careful indeed not to touch the blade with your fingers. You are unlikely to cause yourself any serious injury, but a cut from a fretsaw blade can be very painful, and it is diffi-cult to carry out delicate work when your finger tips are covered in plasters. Some marquetry-cutters will wear a sewing thimble on the finger nearest the blade, sometimes with a small flat piece of wood glued to it to help keep the veneer in contact with the cutting table.

Hold the fretsaw so that you are facing the work and you cut away from yourself. Some people tend to steady the bow of the saw against their shoulder for extra control – you must experiment and find out what is comfortable for you; there are no rules – if it works for you, then it's right. The most difficult thing I had to get used to when I was first learning to use a fretsaw was keeping the saw in one place and moving the work into it – every other type of sawing I had done involved holding the work still and moving the saw along as the cut progressed. You must get used to manoeuvring the work and not the saw, watch the blade carefully and see that the line you are following always meets the blade at right-angles. Watch the line you are following just in front of the blade itself; this part of the design should always be perfectly in line with the blade, no matter whether you are cutting a straight or intricately curved line.

With this flatbed technique of cutting the two contrasting veneers together, you will end up with a picture made up of inserts that exactly fit into the background. They will be exactly the right shape because they were cut together. However, there will of course be a gap between insert and background, because the saw-cut will have destroyed a certain amount of timber, corresponding to its own width. Therefore the finer the blade used for cutting, the smaller will be the gap between your veneers. This gap can of course be filled with a stopper, or grain filler, and can in some instances be just what you want – you may for instance, want to use a contrasting filler to pick out the joints between the veneers. Most often, however, you will want as fine a joint between veneers as possible. The picture, once cut out and the layers of veneer separated, will need to be assembled on a flat surface and glued to a backing paper face-side down, ready to be glued onto its groundwork. The best way to achieve this is to stretch the backing paper over a flat surface and tape or pin it in place, so that the pieces of cut veneer can be laid onto it, with either a little cow gum or Copydex. The pieces of veneer will need to be laid onto the paper accurately, with the gap between background and insert even all the way around.

FLATBED TECHNIQUE: ANOTHER OPTION

When we talked about the flatbed method of cutting, we saw that if the gap between the veneers was to be of an acceptable thickness, we would have to use a very fine blade and accept the fact that at least while we are still novices, we will spend a lot of time fitting new blades after breakage. However, when we have mastered the use of the fretsaw and feel confident in being able to follow a line very accurately, there is another technique that we can employ. Up until now we have always assumed that we will actually cut the line we are following, removing all trace of it in the process. Those of you, who, like me, have had the benefit of at least some formal woodwork tuition will no doubt remember your woodwork teacher continually telling you to cut on the waste side of the line, and that is exactly what we can do. If, instead of cutting out the background and the insert together, we were to cut them out in two separate operations, we would be able to cut on the waste side of the line and make our old woodwork masters very happy.

This technique does call for some very accurate cutting, and we need to have a copy of the appropriate part of the design for each piece being cut. Each separate part of the design will need to have its veneer fixed to a waster veneer at the bottom, to take the rag of the saw and give some extra support, and each piece will need to have the outline of that part of the design pasted on top to follow.

Take one complete paper copy of the design and mark on it what veneer is required for each piece and draw an arrow on each segment to indicate the direction of the grain. Now carefully cut out all the various components with a knife, and keep them in order on a baize-covered tray. Make up the necessary packets of veneer and paste the cut-out sections of drawing onto the appropriate packet of veneer, making sure that the grain direction is correct.

When cutting out the various pieces of veneer, we keep to the outside of the line when cutting pieces to be inserted, and the inside of the line when cutting the background.

As the various pieces are cut out, they must be kept in such a way that they can be easily assembled in their correct place in the design. When assembling the final picture it is best to do so on a reverse copy of the design; this copy needs to be fixed down on a flat surface so that the various components of the design can be placed on it and glued together, starting with the background and working towards the centre.

THE TILTED BED

We have seen how when fretsawing on a flat table, we need to use a very fine blade in order to keep to a minimum the gap around each inserted piece of veneer, but there is a way, if we are only cutting two veneers, of eliminating the gap completely. The method of achieving this is simply to tilt the table on which the veneers are cut.

Prepare your sandwich of two veneers in exactly the same way as just described for

The design drawn out on paper.

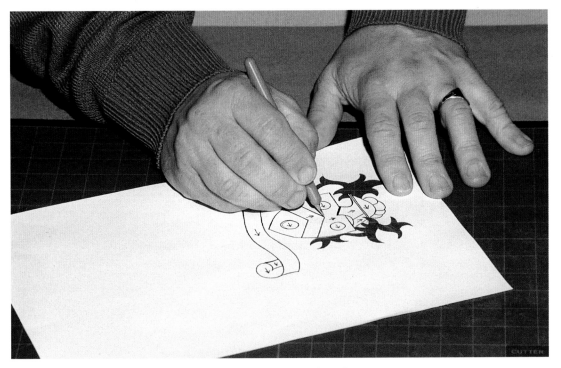

The paper pattern cut into sections and showing grain direction.

The segments arranged on the tray.

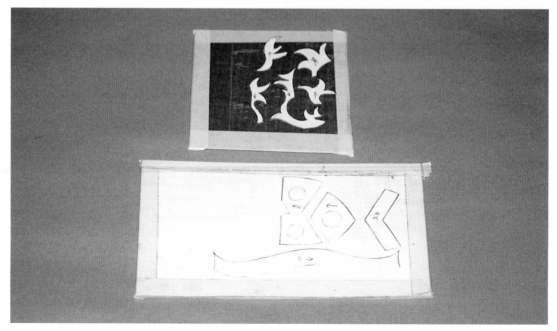

Paste the section of pattern onto the veneer packet.

Cut on the waste side of the line.

the flat bed technique, but tilt the table on which the veneers are being cut by just the right angle. When cut in this way the insert will fit exactly into the background, with no gap at all between the two. This can be better understood by referring to Fig. 10. The top part of section A shows the two veneers joined together for cutting with the fretsaw blade itself cutting through them. The bottom part of section A shows the insert in place in the background and the gap left by the blade as a consequence of cutting on a flat table – it can be seen clearly that a very fine blade is required if this technique is to be employed. Section B on the other hand shows how, if the bed is tilted by exactly the right amount, the gap can be eliminated. Lines D–E and F–G represent the fretsaw blade. It can be seen that in this case, the sloping gap between the top of the veneer at K and the bottom of the veneer at J will

The cut sections waiting to be inserted into the background.

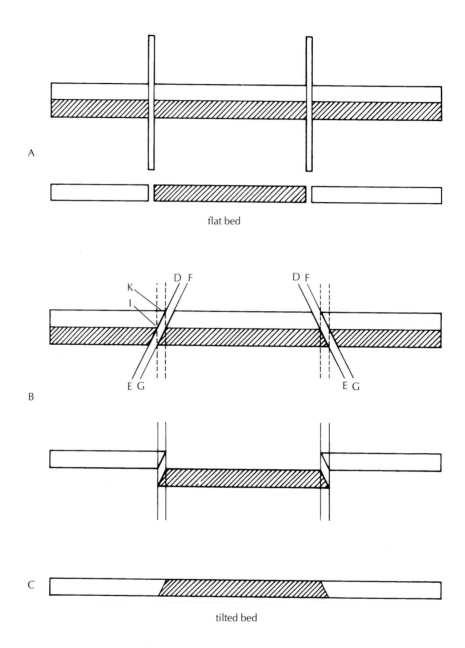

A

flat bed

B

C

tilted bed

The sizes and angles have been exaggerated
in order to show the effect more clearly.

Fig 10 By tilting the bed, all gaps are eliminated.

The finished picture.

eventually be filled by the corresponding slope of the bottom veneer. 'That's easy for you to say', I hear you cry; the lines are somewhat confusing. Hopefully the bottom drawing of section B and section C will show the eventual outcome more clearly.

When employing the tilted or sloping bed for cutting your marquetry, you must remember to keep cutting in the same direction as you started, no matter how many times you have to stop and reinsert the blade. If you are working, for instance, on a table that is tilted the desired amount to the left, and you feed your work into the blade in a clockwise direction, the insert will have to be let in from above. If you feed your work into the blade anticlockwise it will be let in from underneath. The opposite is true if you work on a table that is tilted to the right, and if that has not confused you, remember that we are talking here about a hand-held fretsaw that will have its

teeth facing away from you. Electric fretsaws will have their teeth facing you when you work and all that I have just said will be reversed. Overleaf is a table that you can keep by your saw for reference.

When setting up the tilt of the table in order to cut the veneers in this way, you will have to do so by trial and error. Place two veneers on the table and cut out a simple shape, separate the veneers after cutting and try them together to see how much the gap between them has been reduced. If there is still some gap, then the table needs to be tilted a little more; if they do not fit together then the tilt of the table will need to be reduced. Keep altering the tilt in this way until a perfect fit is obtained and mark the tilt of the table for future reference. The amount of tilt required can be reduced, if need be, by placing an extra layer of waste veneer between the two pieces that are actually wanted.

*Sometimes a picture can be inspired by the grain of a particular
piece of veneer, and this is certainly the case in 'Spirit of Trees'
by W. A. Maestranzi of London.*

Hand-held Saw with Teeth Facing Away from You

Table tilted to the left feeding work into blade clockwise: insert from above.
Table tilted to the left feeding work into blade anticlockwise: insert from underneath.
Table tilted to the right feeding work into blade clockwise: insert from underneath.
Table tilted to the right feeding work into blade anticlockwise: insert from above.

Electric Fretsaw with Teeth Facing Towards You

Table tilted to the left feeding work into blade clockwise: insert from underneath.
Table tilted to the left feeding work into blade anticlockwise: insert from above.
Table tilted to the right feeding work into blade clockwise: insert from above
Table tilted to the right feeding work into blade anticlockwise: insert from underneath.

THE PATCH METHOD (FLATBED)

In this method of marquetry-cutting the entire picture can be cut in one operation, and the result will be a perfect fit to within the thickness of the blade used. The finer the blade, of course, the smaller the gap between components. You will first need to obtain several easy-to-cut veneers, such as sycamore, to use as wasters, and a couple of copies of the overall design, one of which should be reversed. The idea is to make up a sandwich of waster veneers with the chosen veneers for the design let in to them as patches in the appropriate places, veneers that are adjacent to each other in the design will have to be let into different wasters, but ideally will be in the next layer in the sandwich. In many pictures it will of course be possible to use one of the background veneers, such as the sky or sea, as a

waster itself. Most pictures should be capable of being cut from a sandwich of five or six layers, but if the picture requires any more than this it would be a good idea to make up more than one sandwich. The most important part of making up the patches, is of course, to be sure that you get them in exactly the right place in the waster for cutting, and the best way to achieve this is to first, make sure that all the wasters are exactly the same size, and secondly to draw cross-hairs across the centre with registration marks so that all the layers can be lined up exactly when being fixed together.

Have one of your master drawings photocopied onto a transparent sheet, to be used as a kind of 'finder' so that you can hold it over the piece of veneer you are considering using and yet be able to clearly see the veneer underneath. In this way you can be sure to select just the right piece of veneer and grain for the job. Cut out the piece of chosen veneer oversize and in a

Patched veneers ready for Wheal Coats.

rectangular, square, or triangular shape, that can easily be let into the waster, leaving an area of waste around the edge, approximately 5 to 10mm in size, depending on the size of the patch itself. Next, place the finder on to the waster veneer, making sure that it is in the correct position by lining up the cross-hairs and register marks. Slip the patch of veneer you have just cut out between the finder and the waster, so that it is in the correct position, and draw a pencil line around the edge of the patch. Transfer the waster to the cutting mat, cut out the shape of the patch to be inserted and then fix the patch in place with a little glue on the edges, or some veneer tape on the back. Fix as many patches into each waster as you can, but remember that pieces of veneer that butt against one another in the actual picture will have to be patched in different wasters, although it is also a good idea to make sure, if possible, that they are in the next layer of the sandwich, as the further apart they are when being cut the more chance there is of error due to the fretsaw blade not being held perfectly upright.

When all the wasters have been patched in this way, they will need to be held together for cutting, and this can be done in one of several ways. You can apply a little dab of Copydex or cow gum; alternatively you can either staple or pin the layers together with office staples or veneer pins, or you can hold the layers together with masking tape around the edges. It is always best to put a block of wood either side of the sandwich of veneers and cramp them tightly together when taping the edges together

If we look again at Wheal Coats enginehouse, the picture can be completed with five layers. The first waster is made up of the veneers for the cliff in the foreground and the sky, together with patches for the sea and the door in the front wall of the engine-house. The second waster has patches for the chimney, the front wall and

the white slope of the cliffs. The third has the far cliff, the beach, the back wall and the collar of the chimney. The fourth has the side cliff and the side walls. The remaining waster is the veneer for the far shore and has in it the patch for the top of the walls. This is only one way of organizing the patches and layers for this picture – there are others, and it would be a good exercise for you to try and find these other, possibly better ways. The things to look for, remember, are to get as many patches in one waster as possible, without having pieces in the same waster that are adjacent to each other in the picture. See how many different ways you can find of patching the wasters for this picture, and decide for yourself which is the best.

When it comes to cutting the veneer sandwich you will have to make holes with a pricker or Archimedean drill at various places in order to insert the fretsaw blade. Make these holes as few as possible and choose a position for them at corners or places where the line to be followed alters direction sharply, so that they will be less obvious in the final picture. Use as fine a blade as you can, and keep the saw as upright as possible.

When the cutting is complete, the various parts can be assembled face down on a reversed copy of the design to ensure that whatever gap there is between pieces, is evenly spaced around each piece. This spacing can be done either by applying a little glue to the surface of the veneer and assembling the picture like a jigsaw, or by securing a piece of self adhesive film over a flat surface, sticky side up, and assembling the pieces on that. Once the picture is assembled in this way, the side facing you can be sanded lightly to ensure that it is clean and flat, ready to be glued to the groundwork. After laying, the reversed copy of the picture is removed and the front of the marquetry can be prepared for finishing.

WINDOW METHOD WITH FRETSAW

In this method you start off with a waste veneer in exactly the same way as for the knife cut window technique. The design is placed over the waster with the carbon paper beneath and the design marked out; however, this time a small hole is made so that the blade can be inserted to cut out the window, and the window itself is cut undersize, indeed, the cut need not even follow the contours of the design as the only reason the window is cut out, is to enable you to place the chosen veneer underneath the window in order to select the right area of grain. When the position of the veneer to be inserted has been finally established, a mark is made in pencil to enable you to place it back in the same position again. The design for that particular piece is then transferred to the insert veneer and this is then placed on the cutting table and cut out oversize: I recommend that a good 20mm be left all round. When this has been done the insert veneer is once again placed under the window and secured in the correct position with a little glue. A small hole is made through both thicknesses of veneer on the line of the pattern, the blade is inserted and the window and the insert veneer are cut out together on a tilted table to ensure a close fit. The offcuts of veneers from both window and inserts are carefully removed and the

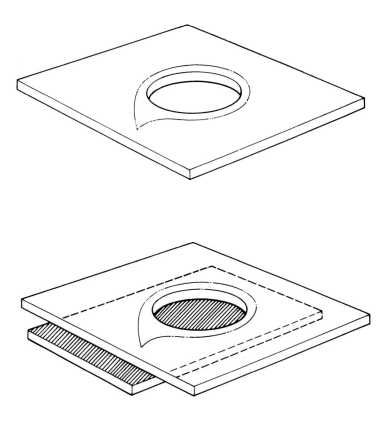

Fig 11 Top: the window cut out. Bottom: veneer fixed underneath for cutting.

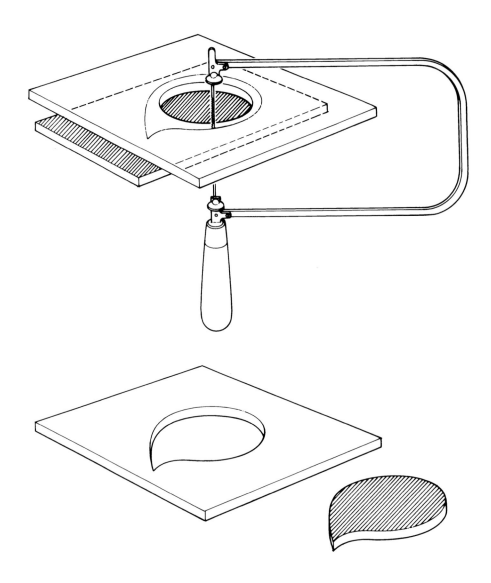

Fig 12 Top: fretsawing the window. Bottom: window and insert cut out.

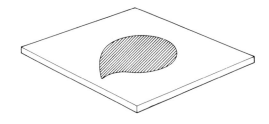

Fig 13 Insert in place.

inserted piece of veneer is fitted in place with a little glue on the edges just as before. The next piece of the design can then have its window cut out undersize and the process repeated. It is possible to cut out several windows at a time as long as they are not adjacent to one another, and it is possible to insert pieces from above or below, depending on the tilt of the table.

PIECE BY PIECE

THE DRAWING

The technique of using a perforated drawing to reproduce a quantity of exact designs is still in use today. In the past, the pricking of the holes was done with a treadle-driven device that looked a little like an old-fashioned dentist's drill. Today of course the marquetarian has the advantage of a motor-driven machine, with a rheostat that allows the speed to be controlled. The holes must be made close enough together to form a continuous line, but too fast a speed on the machine can tear the paper. To produce the copy, place a sheet of paper underneath the perforated drawing and rub gently over the surface with a pad coated in Judaean bitumen. This is a very fine powder that penetrates the perforations and is deposited on the paper beneath. The paper is then heated to secure the design and the process can be repeated as often as required.

Photocopying is another process that can be used for smaller designs. Printing was also used to some extent in the eighteenth century, when a large number of copies of a small motif were constantly required.

THE VENEERS

The individual elements of the design are all cut out separately from packets of veneer. A large professional workshop will have a supply of veneer packets ready made up for use by the marquetry-cutter, with the type of veneer and the grain direction marked on them. These packets consist of several layers of veneer with a piece of greased paper between every fourth or fifth layer to lubricate the saw blade during cutting.

The various parts of the paper pattern are cut out with a knife and placed on the marquetry-cutter's shelf, according to their position in the design. If the direction of the grain is important, then this is marked on the paper. The pieces of paper are then glued onto the appropriate packet of veneers for cutting. When the pieces are cut out, the saw is kept to the outside of the line, but obliterating it.

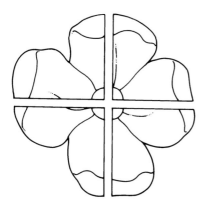

Paper pattern is cut into four when pasted to the veneer for cutting.

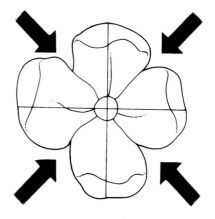

After cutting the petals out the pieces can be joined with little or no gap.

Fig 14 Pattern cut into four.

If a piece such as a flower, or other item that is made up of individual pieces of the same veneer, is to be cut, all the inner petals will need to be cut out before the overall silhouette. To compensate for the spaces left by the kerf of the saw during cutting the paper pattern is cut into four and glued onto the veneer packet with a space left between the four sections. The pieces are cut with the saw centre line, and if the correct space has been left between the four sections the piece should fit together in the background with very little gap between segments as can be seen in Fig 14.

The cut pieces are arranged on the marquetry-cutter's shelf and the layers in the packets are separated ready for inlaying. If any sand shading is required, then this is the time for it to be carried out; any engraving can be done after the picture is completed.

BACKGROUND

The background into which the marquetry picture is fitted could of course simply be a sheet of plain veneer, but more often than not it will be made up of quartered veneers with a border of some kind, or it could possibly even be a piece of parquetry.

The various options shown here can be used both for the back of marquetry panels or as we are discussing here, for the background into which to inlay a marquetry picture.

- **Slip matching**: This simply means taking a number of sequential sheets of veneer and slipping them sideways for jointing.
- **Book matching**: In book matching, pairs of veneer sheets are opened as the pages of a book and jointed.
- **Four-way match (quartered top)**: The first two sequential sheets are opened

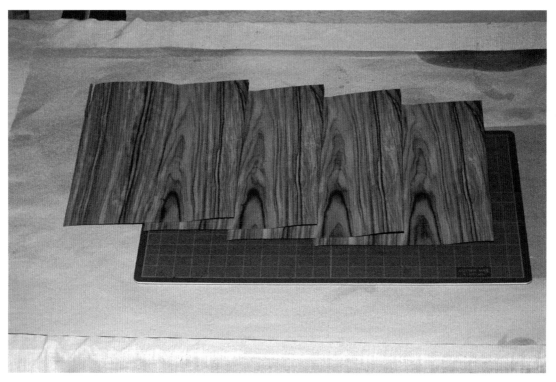

Slip matching.

Book matching.

Four-way match.

book fashion as for book matching. The second two sequential sheets are opened in the same way, but are then flipped over on their horizontal axis.

- **Diamond match**: Take four veneers and cut them into a rhomboid shape and then open them in a book match. Using a straight edge, cut off the triangular ends and bring the top triangle down to form a rectangle with the bottom off-cut. Move the bottom triangle up to form a rectangle with the top off-cut.
- **Diagonal square**: Four veneers are cut into triangles and jointed as shown. The angle of the joint will vary depending on whether the panel is a square or rectangle.
- **Diagonal cross**: This is the same as with the diagonal square, except that the triangles are cut across the grain.
- **Butterfly wings**: Some veneers can be matched to form butterfly wings, as shown in Fig 15.

- **Parquetry**: Diamonds, Louis cube, trellis or any other form of parquetry can also be used very effectively as a background. See section on parquetry for examples.

Any or all of these various backgrounds can have bandings or borders around the edge.

When the background is completed it must have a paper backing glued on to give it support and it must have a veneer mounted on each side to protect it during cutting. One copy of the design is glued onto the top veneer before the sandwich is made up, and is then cut to the exact size, so that it can be positioned exactly on the background. It is probable that more than one panel will be required and so a packet of backgrounds for cutting would be made up. The packet of veneers is cramped together, possibly with veneer pins in strategic places to prevent slipping, and the edges would be secured with glue or tape.

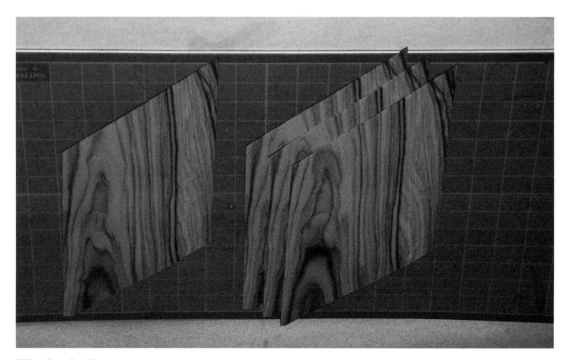

The rhomboid.

Book match the rhomboid shape.

Cut off the triangular ends.

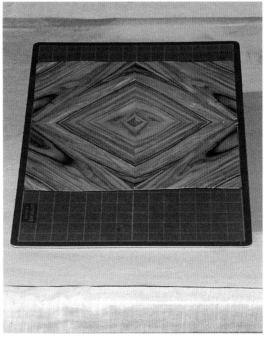

Interchange the triangle sections.

Diagonal square.

Diagonal cross.

Fig 15 Butterfly wings.

The background is cut with the saw blade to the inside of the line, but obliterating it. When the background is cut out it is possible that it will warp or distort, making it difficult to fit in the inserts. For this reason, inlaying the various parts of the design begins immediately. If the design is large with a lot of parts to be inlayed, the marquetry-cutter will leave small braces in the background when he cuts it out. These small braces or stops in the cutting help to stop the background from distorting after cutting, and are removed just prior to that particular piece being inlaid.

three

TINTING AND SHADING

STAINED VENEERS

The artist who uses paint, be it water colour or oil, is in the enviable position of having a full palette of colours to draw from, and can lighten or darken them at will, or even mix them together to form completely new colours. The marquetarian on the other hand has a very restricted palette and no means of mixing new colours: he has to work with what nature has given, and some would say that to increase the options open to him by staining or bleaching defeats what the marquetarian is striving to achieve – a picture created from natural materials. However, others, myself included, will argue that the tinting or shading of wood veneers complements and increases the scope of the marquetarian by completing the spectrum, and making available colours that could not otherwise be used. No one would suggest that it is acceptable simply to take any nondescript piece of veneer

Sand shading.

The result of sand shading.

and stain it to the required colour, regardless of whether or not it is possible to obtain other veneers that would do the job – you might as well simply paint the picture, if that is what you want to achieve; but by the same token, it would be a shame to spoil a work simply because the colour you require is not naturally available. So remember that staining should only be used if there is no acceptable alternative.

Stained veneers are readily available from your marquetry supplier.

SHADING

Most marquetry pictures will require some shading in order to portray solidity, curves, contours and shadows, and the most usual method of shading is with the use of hot sand. Fine silver sand is used, heated in a shallow saucepan or baking tray to a depth of about 50mm or so. There are two ways in which the sand can be used. If it is the edge

of the veneer that needs to be shaded then the piece in question can be held with a pair of tweezers and inserted into the sand to the desired depth, this will give a graduated effect as the part of the veneer that is deepest in the sand will emerge darker. If the edge is concave, as with a crescent, for instance, and you want the shading to be even over the length of the curve, then it is a good idea to pile the sand up into a mound that matches the curve of the veneer so that the whole length is inserted into the sand to the same depth, rather then have the points of the crescent going in deeper than the centre and therefore shading that much more than the centre. Keep the sand at a constant temperature so that you can try a few pieces as testers before shading the actual piece to be used. Do not hold the veneer in the sand too long in one go – take it out and check it for colour, it can always be reinserted if it needs more treatment. Darker veneers will take longer to shade than light ones and may require the sand to be at a greater temperature. When the desired effect has been achieved, wipe the veneer with a damp clean rag to replace some of the moisture that will have been lost and allow it to dry under a weight to keep it flat, before being assembled in the picture.

If the area of the veneer you wish to shade is in the centre of a veneer segment rather than the edge, then you will have to spoon the hot sand onto the veneer. The area of veneer that does not require shading can be protected from the hot sand either with a cardboard template or by being given a coat of polish on the areas that are not to be shaded. The veneer is then held with tweezers over the sand tray and spoonfuls of the hot sand are poured over it until the desired effect is obtained.

Another method of shading the veneer is to place it on a hot plate; this can also be used in conjunction with a household iron and is ideal if you wish to shade a large piece of veneer, perhaps to be used for a sky effect. You may wish to shade a larger piece of veneer in this way before it is cut to shape, and then place the veneer under your window and select the best area to use.

PYROGRAPHY

The Victorians were great ones for decorating furniture in a variety of different ways, and one method that they used was Pokerwork. A hot poker or soldering iron was used to burn or scorch a picture or pattern into the wood. Pyrography, as this artform should more properly be called, can also be used to shade areas on your marquetry picture or to put in details after the veneers have been laid. It is possible to purchase special pyrography tools with interchangeable points, or you can make you own assortment of metal tools from old files and heat them with a blowtorch. The difficulty if you make your own tools is in maintaining a constant temperature, but practice and experience will overcome this.

ENGRAVING

Some of the antique marquetry that you will see in stately homes or museums, will have some of the fine detail engraved in the lighter veneers and picked out with dark wax or Indian ink. This method of engraving was also used as an alternative to sand shading on light veneers, where the area to be shaded was either crosshatched or just had one or two straight lines engraved to represent shadow.

BLEACHING

There are several preparatory bleaches that can be purchased from French polishers' suppliers or you can obtain oxalic acid crystals, but the two I use most often are Cloros laundry bleach or hydrogen peroxide. Cloros was very easy to obtain at one time, but now you have to shop around for it. You can try other bleaches but I have always found Cloros to be the best. Hydrogen peroxide 100 vol is something you will have to ask a chemist to get for you. Please remember that whatever bleach you are using it will necessary to take some precautions: always wear safety glasses and avoid contact with the skin.

LAUNDRY BLEACH

Each piece of veneer that is to be bleached will have to be treated before it is included in the picture. The bleach itself must held in a plastic or glass container with a big enough neck for the piece of veneer that is to be bleached to be held inside with tweezers. Each time you come to bleach a given piece of veneer, always try one or two pieces first, and observe the effect, before attempting the actual piece to be used. Cut several pieces the same shape and size as the one to be used and hold one of these in the bleach

Engraving: close-up of an Anglo-Indian toilet mirror of c.1785.

with tweezers, timing how long it is immersed. Take the veneer out of the bleach and examine it: if it has not lightened enough, try another piece for longer. Continue in this way, timing each piece until you have achieved the desired effect. In this way you can be confident that you will get the result you want with the piece you intend to use.

It is important, once the veneer has been bleached to the correct shade, that the effects of the bleach should be neutralized by rinsing well with water and the veneer should then be allowed to dry between sheets of newspaper and under flat boards before being fitted into the picture.

HYDROGEN PEROXIDE 100 VOL

This is much stronger than the peroxide used to bleach hair, which is probably no more than 11 vol so be very careful and take full precautions: you do not want this on your skin! Basically the procedure is exactly the same as that used for laundry bleach – timing is all important, and neutralize with water the same way.

Hydrogen peroxide must be stored in the dark or it will lose its strength.

BANDINGS AND FILLETS

Decorative bandings are available from veneer suppliers, and vary in complexity of design from simple boxwood or black lines known as 'stringing' to different coloured herringbone bandings or diamond and key patterns, together with various cross-banded woods with lined edges. These bandings can be used to finish off the edge of a picture, either before the border, or just a little into the border, as in the portrait of John Major by F. L. Holmes, shown in the Gallery, but you must be careful in your selection of banding – if you are going to use one, you do not want it to detract from the effect of the picture itself: choose something subtle and in keeping with the theme or mood of the picture. A quiet country cottage would not appreciate being surrounded by a tulipwood and boxwood 10mm-wide banding, or a Grecian key – far better to go for a narrow walnut feather, and keep the more flamboyant bandings for a carnival scene. 'Spirit of the Trees' by W. A. Maestranzi, also in the Gallery, shows a nice touch by including a small detail in the top left-hand corner of the border.

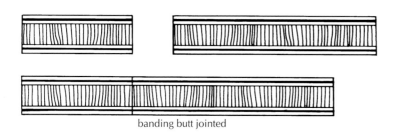

banding butt jointed

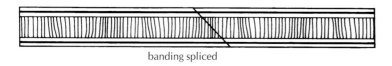

banding spliced

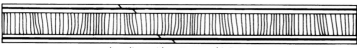

banding with a staggered joint

Fig 16 Step jointing.

JOINTING

Fillets and banding are normally purchased in one-metre lengths, which will be long enough for most pictures and they will not need to be jointed, other than at a mitred corner or other natural junction, unless you are making a very large panel indeed, or you are using up some off-cuts or possibly restoring an old panel. When a time comes that a joint has to be made in the length of a run of banding, the choice of joint will depend on the style of banding being used. Obviously a straight stringing will be best jointed with a simple splice, but such a splice may show if made on a banding that has a cross-banded centre. With a cross-banded edging it may be better to use a stepped joint. Cut the outer stringings on one side with a 45-degree splice. Then cut straight across the cross-banded section in line with the grain a little way on and then

again a little further on cut the stringing on the other side with a splice.

BORDERS

The simplest way to make your borders is to cut four strips from a sheet of straight-grained veneer, and fit them around the edge of your picture with a mitre at each corner. If you have fitted a banding or fillet around the picture it is very important that the mitres match up – nothing looks worse or more amateurish than mitres that don't quite coincide. The best way to achieve this is to tape the banding and border together and treat them as one, cutting the mitres together in one operation.

If you want to make the borders a little more elaborate, you can use a burr veneer, or if you have enough veneer, you can match them in the following way. Select two

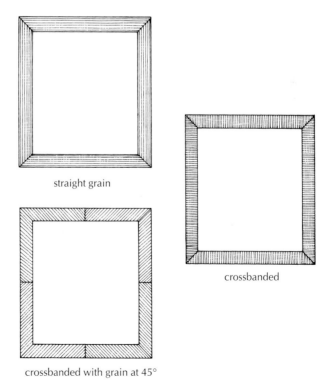

straight grain

crossbanded

crossbanded with grain at 45°

Fig 17 Borders.

Draw the outline with a fine pencil.

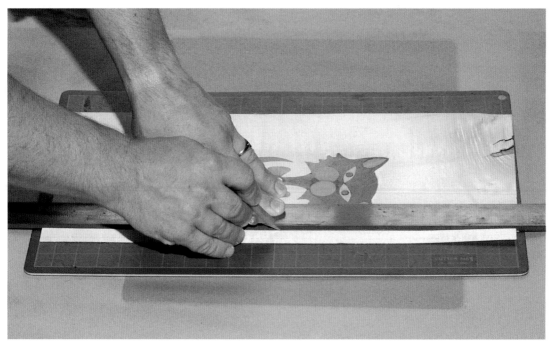

Use a straight edge for cutting.

consecutive veneers, and cut through the two strips together to obtain the two edge strips, open them out as if you were opening the pages of a book, keeping the most decorative edge of the veneer as the centre. One side will be the mirror image of the other, and the top and bottom borders can be cut in the same manner. Another way of cutting the borders is to have them cross-banded, so that the grain is at right-angles to the edge of the board all the way round, any joints in the sides or the top and bottom can be shot at 90 degrees on the shooting board, the corners will of course be mitred and produce a nice feathered effect (*see* Fig 17). The cross-banding can be made more elaborate by putting a joint in the centre of each border and cutting the veneer so that the grain is at a 45-degree angle to the edge, matching the angle of the corner mitre and forming a feather effect that draws the eye in towards the picture. This is also an effective way to cross-band the border if the veneer you choose for this purpose does not have a straight grain.

FITTING THE BORDERS

In order to fit any bandings and borders, the picture must be trimmed to the correct finished size. Place the picture face-side down on a flat surface and draw in the edges of your picture with a fine pencil. Double-check that the rectangle you draw has 90-degree angles and that your picture is centred and upright. One of the best ways of checking that a rectangle has square corners, is to measure the distances across the two diagonals: if the rectangle is true, then these two measurements will be exactly the same. When you are quite sure you have it right, check it again: only then cut your picture to size. When cutting, use a long stroke against a straight edge, with the knife handle held low. Cut away from the corners and do not try to cut through in one go: make a scoring cut first, just as when cutting your

picture components. You may prefer to cut around the picture with a veneer saw against the straight edge, but you will have to be careful not to break bits out at the corners.

Cut your borders and bandings a little over-size in length and tape them to the edges of your picture, leaving the ends to overlap at the corners. Still working from the back of your picture, mark the mitres at each corner, ensuring that they are exactly 45 degrees and that they exactly meet the corner of the picture. Again use a straight edge and cut the mitres; in order to avoid splitting the grain you should cut from the outer edge towards the picture. Do not try to cut through both layers at once, and if you can, use a bevelled cut, to obtain a square butt joint. Once cut, a little tape will protect the points.

GROUNDWORK

Once the picture is cut to size and any borders have been fitted we can turn our attention to the groundwork on which the picture is to be laid. The first thing we have to decide is, what material are we going to use?

MATERIALS FOR GROUNDWORK

Wood

Antique marquetry was of course always laid on solid wood. This was done not from choice, but because nothing better was available. As a base-board of solid wood has many disadvantages: it shrinks, it can crack, and the very act of veneering on it will cause it to warp. If you do need to lay your veneers on solid timber, then American oak or straight-grained mahogany are to be recommended. Remember that if one side of the board only is to be veneered, then you should always lay the veneer on the side that was next to the heartwood, as this will help to counteract the natural

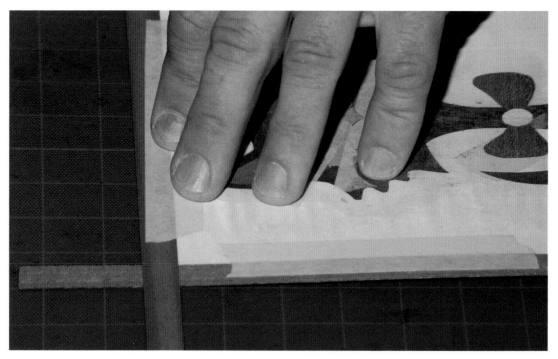

Leave the corners to overlap.

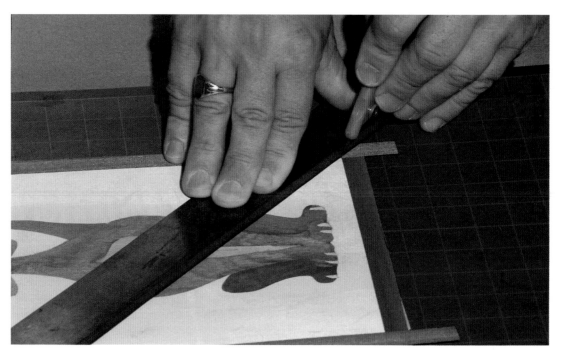

Cutting the mitres.

Heartwood side nearest to centre of tree veneer should be laid this side.

Board cut into five with every other piece turned over to counteract tendency for board to warp.

Fig 18a Veneer is laid on heartwood side.

Fig 18b Every other piece is reversed to prevent warping.

tendency for the board to warp so that the heartwood presents itself on the convex. You can determine which was the heartwood side by examining the end of the board: the annual growth rings will show which side was nearest the centre of the tree. If both sides are to be veneered, then the usual practice is to cut the board into narrow strips and glue them back together with every other strip turned over.

Another problem that may arise with timber is imperfections such as knots, or in the case of reclaimed or second-hand timber, which will be better seasoned than new, old screw- or nail-holes. Any screwholes will have to be filled, and indeed it would be preferable to remove any knots and fill these holes as well. There are all sorts of preparatory fillers on the market which state that you can glue onto them, and while I do not doubt this claim in any way, I feel it is far better to fill any hole with timber of the same kind you are using – use pine to fill pine, mahogany to fill mahogany and so on.

The piece of wood you use to fill the hole needs to have the grain running the same way as that of the wood you are filling – it is no good chamfering down a piece of wood and filling the hole with it on end grain, or using a piece of dowel. There are two good reasons why this practice is to be avoided: first, the glue will not stick so well to end grain and you could end up with a bubble in the veneer at a later stage, and secondly, if the wood on which you have laid your veneer shrinks at

all over the years, the piece you used to fill the hole will end up proud of the surface and cause the veneer to lift. So always use a piece of similar timber and inlay it in the surface with long grain. There are plug cutters on the market that cut a perfectly round wooden plug for hole filling which are ideal for this purpose.

Once any holes and other imperfections on the surface have been dealt with, the timber side to be veneered should be planed with a toothing plane, in order to give a good key for the glue and also to ensure that the surface is perfectly flat (*see* page 13). Plane the surface at 45 degrees in both directions and then end up going with the grain. Make sure that you keep the plane flat on the surface, especially near the edges, as you do not want to tip the plane and take off the edge of the panel. If the panel is to be veneered on the edges as well as the face, then the edge veneers should be applied first; these can either be dealt with in the same way as the face or you can use some iron-on strip.

Chipboard
Chipboard is much better than timber for laying your picture on, but even this is not immune from warping. Make sure you use a piece of a suitable thickness for the size of your picture, and always veneer both sides. When gluing on chipboard you will find it advantageous to size the board with a solution of diluted glue. Allow the size to dry fully before sanding down the surface

ready for gluing. The edges of chipboard are best capped with timber to give them some strength, rather than just veneering them. See below.

Blockboard and Plywood

I have put these two boards together because there is little if anything to choose between them for our purpose. It is customary when ordering boards of this type to specify the dimension that is with the grain of the top layer. A panel that is 100 by 200 will have the grain running in the 100 direction, whereas a panel that is 200 by 100 will have the top grain running in the 200 direction.

MDF

MDF is by far the best material to use for marquetry pictures, but I would still urge you to veneer both sides, and not to skimp on thickness if you are undertaking a large picture.

PREPARATION OF GROUNDWORK

Prior to laying the veneer, some preparation of the groundwork will be necessary. First you must ensure that it is perfectly flat, and this can be achieved by trying a straight edge on the surface. If you are using a solid wooden panel that needs to be made flat, you will need to make up a panel jig. A panel jig is simply a plywood or other flat board on which the panel can be placed, and has strips of wood that are thinner than the panel pinned around the edges, so that the panel can be held fast and planed. The jig itself can be cramped to a table or bench. Two parallel strips of timber known as winding sticks are placed across the panel, one at each end. By sighting across the top of the two winding sticks, it is possible to determine whether or not the panel is flat and if not, where the panel needs to be planed.

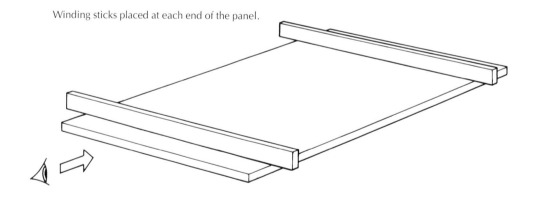
Winding sticks placed at each end of the panel.

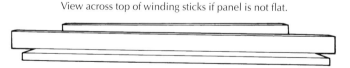
View across top of winding sticks if panel is not flat.

Fig 19 Winding sticks.

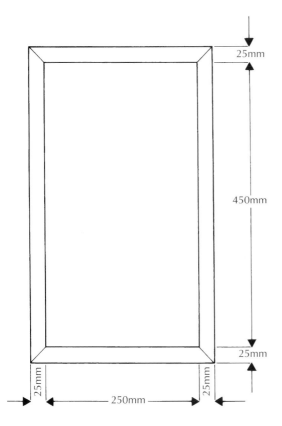

Fig 20 Calculating the size of the groundwork.

If you are laying your veneers on boards other than chipboard, the groundwork should be gone over with a toothing plane. The toothing plane provides a key for the glue and will also remove any unseen high spots. The panel should of course be held in the panel jig for this operation.

When laying veneers on chipboard it is advisable to treat the groundwork with a glue size, because the surface of chipboard is very absorbent. Dilute some glue by eight parts to one with water and spread this on the surface. Allow the size to dry overnight and then sand down using a medium paper and a sanding block before laying the veneer.

CUTTING THE GROUNDWORK

When you have decided on a material for the groundwork, the next job is to cut it to size. The groundwork must be cut to exactly the size of the finished picture, including the border. If the groundwork is to have a lipping applied to the edges under the veneer, then it will need to be first cut undersize to allow for the width of the lippings. If, for instance, the picture, including any banding and border is to be 300mm wide and 500mm in height and the lippings are 25mm wide, then the groundwork will have to be 250mm wide by 450mm in height.

Cut out this rectangle and plane the edges. Now turn your picture upside down and place the undersize groundwork on it. You should be able to position it so that the mitres of your picture bandings line up with the corners of the groundwork. If this is the case then you can carry on and fit the lippings.

THE BACK OF THE GROUNDWORK

The back of your base board can be veneered with an ordinary straight-grained veneer. As it will probably be hung on a wall and never seen, this should suffice, but most marquetarians take a pride in finishing off their work in style, and many backs will be quartered or diamond matched.

EDGE LIPPINGS OR CAPPING STRIPS

It is not usually suitable simply to veneer the edge of a panel, especially if you are using chipboard; it is far better to edge with a wooden lipping. If you intend the front of the panel to be flat right to the edge, as is the usual practice, then it is far

Some people say that all you ever see of any politician is a veneer. Well this is certainly the case with this portrait 'John Major' by F. L. Holmes of Bournemouth.

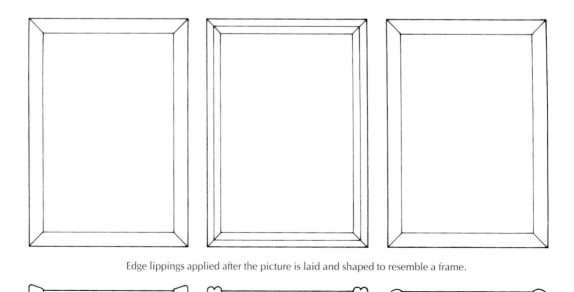

Edge lippings applied after the picture is laid and shaped to resemble a frame.

Fig 21 Capping strips shaped to resemble a frame.

Lippings are cut to size.

Lipping kept in order against a straight edge

better to apply the lippings before the panel is veneered, in order to avoid having to level the front of the lipping to the front of an already laid picture. However if you apply the lipping after the marquetry is laid, it is possible to make a feature of it, by having the front of the lipping proud of the panel, and perhaps shaped like a frame (*see* Fig 21). If you do decide to apply the lipping after you have laid the picture, in order to have it stand proud, then you may want to consider polishing the picture first as well, as it will be difficult to get properly into the corners once the frame or lipping is in place.

APPLYING LIPPINGS

To attach the lipping to the edge of the panel, you have several options. If the lipping is on solid wood or MDF, it will be sufficient to glue it in place, possibly using the odd pin as follows. Cut the four pieces of lipping exactly to size with a mitre at each corner. Mark the corners that go together and place them in a line against a straight edge with the outer edges uppermost and the corners touching. Now stretch a piece of good-quality masking tape across each joint and stick down firmly. Turn the assembly over and apply

Apply glue.

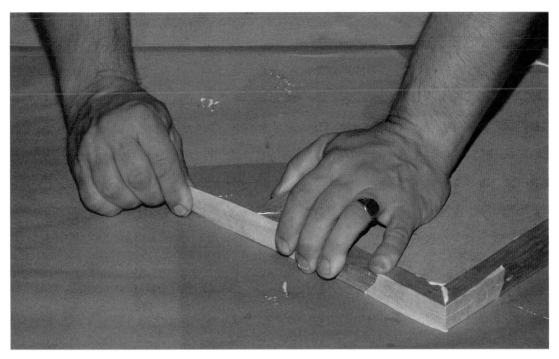

The final mitre held.

Extra masking tape applied to ensure firm contact.

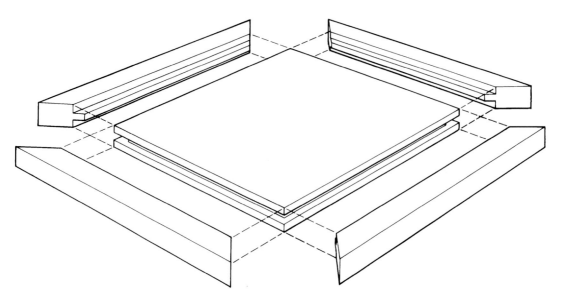

Fig 22 Lippings tongued and grooved.

glue to the surfaces. You will find that the four pieces of lipping when lifted, can easily be assembled as a frame around the groundwork and held in place by applying masking tape to the final corner. All that remains to be done now is to stretch some more tape over the lippings as shown, in order to ensure a good contact, and to clean off any excess glue. When the glue is dry, you can put a small pin in the mitre if you wish, or you can put two saw cuts across the joint at a right-angle and insert a slip of veneer into each to prevent the mitre from opening up. For materials other than MDF the lipping should be tongued and grooved (*see* Fig 22). You can achieve this with either a combination plane or an electric router. Cut the groove first, an equal distance from both sides of the panel and one-third of its thickness in width. The easiest way to cut tongues is to work on the edge of the plank of wood that is going to be used for the lippings. Cut the tongue on the edge of the plank just short of the depth of the groove so as to ensure a good snug fit at the shoulders. Be sure that is it a good fit, but not too tight in the groove, as too tight a fit could cause the panel to spread at the edges. After the tongue is cut on the edge of the plank the lipping can be sliced off and the next tongue cut. Cutting the lippings in this way means that you are always working on a piece of wood that is easily held in the vice.

LAYING THE PICTURE

The procedure for laying the back veneers and the picture itself are the same, so the following instruction can be followed for both.

CONTACT ADHESIVE

Contact adhesives such as Evostik give off a dangerous and inflammable vapour and should only be used in a well-ventilated area where there are no naked flames and no one is smoking.

Spread the adhesive thinly onto both surfaces to be joined, and allow to become touch dry before bringing the two surfaces into contact with each other, when they will bond instantly. The comb that is normally supplied with such adhesive for spreading purposes is designed for spreading onto laminates, and will apply far too thick a coat for wood veneer. If you intend to use this method of laying your picture I recommend that you make a spreader of your own with much finer teeth. Spread the adhesive evenly over both surfaces making sure that you cover the whole surface right to the edges without any areas where the glue has pooled or built up, and being careful not to allow any foreign material to fall on the surface during the drying period. Drying times are always given on the tin and should be strictly adhered to, although certain allowances are made for varying room temperatures.

There are two ways in which the surfaces can be brought into contact with one another. You can very carefully position the groundwork over the upturned picture, being careful not to allow them to touch until you are completely sure they are in the correct place, and then carefully press them together. Another way of ensuring correct alignment is to place a sheet of paper between the two surfaces to prevent them touching while you position them – the dried glue will not stick to the paper. When you are sure that you have them in the correct position, slip the paper out a little at a time, pressing the two surfaces together as you do so. Firm pressure is required to ensure that no air gets trapped.

HOT GLUE

If you are determined to try this method out of curiosity, then the back veneer can be laid either by press or hammer, as follows.

HAMMER METHOD

This is suitable only for single sheets of veneer or quartered panels, it is not possible to lay marquetry by this method.

Hot or scotch glue is purchased in cake or pearl form and must be dissolved in water. It is best if the glue is left to soak for some time in cold water before being heated in the inner glue pot. Only enough water to just cover the glue in the pot should be used at first, more being added later as required. Keep the water as hot as possible in the outer pot without allowing it to boil over, and stir the glue at regular intervals. When the glue is ready for use a skin cover will form over the top and it should then be tested for thickness. Pick up some of the glue on the glue brush and allow it to run back into the pot. It should run in a continuous stream with no lumps or thick parts and should not break into droplets. If necessary, more water or glue can be added to get the required consistency. When working with hot glue, speed is of the essence, so everything that is likely to be needed should be prepared beforehand. All blocks, etc. should be got ready and any cramps should be opened to the correct gap. A supply of hot water should be available and all the surfaces to be glued, all tools to be used and all blocks and presses, etc. should be heated prior to use.

The surface to be veneered should have been made as flat as possible and then planed with a toothing plane. After toothing, the groundwork should be treated with a size made of liquid glue mixed with water. Care must be taken to spread the size evenly over the surface and when it is dry any high spots should be removed with the toothing plane. The veneer to be used should be slightly dampened with tepid water and then allowed to dry between two sheets of newspaper and kept flat between two pieces of wood with a weight on top until dry. This will ensure that when you come to use the veneer it is quite flat.

When all has been prepared as described a good layer of glue is spread onto the surface to be veneered and the veneer is positioned in place. Glue is then spread on top of the veneer to act as a lubricant for the veneering hammer. Excess glue is then squeezed out from under the veneer by use of the veneering hammer, which is pulled over the surface at a slight angle to the grain, starting at the centre and working gradually towards the edge squeezing out the glue as it goes. If the glue starts to harden and buckle the veneer it can be reheated with a warm iron. The surface of the veneer must be kept moist at all times by applying glue or size. When the veneer is down, excess glue from the top of the veneer can be cleaned off with a hot damp rag, but care must be taken not to get the surface too wet. Check the whole surface for areas that have failed to stick properly by tapping the surface with your finger – you will be able to tell if it is solid or if the veneer has lifted. If the veneer is not secure, a little more heat can be applied with an iron and the veneer hammered down again; if this fails to solve the problem, it may be necessary to split the veneer with a marquetry knife and insert more glue, hammer down again but this time work towards the cut just made and then a caul or heated block must be cramped over the area, but remember to put at least one sheet of newspaper under the block so that it can be more easily removed when dry.

If two or more pieces of veneer are to be jointed, such as with a quartered top, these are more successfully put down by the caul method, but with care and experience it is possible to put them down with the hammer. Great care must be taken in positioning the veneer so that the joints are in the correct place and the grain matches for a good end result. The veneers are put down as just described but the edges are allowed to overlap and a joint is cut with a chisel, using a straight edge. The chisel is used to cut through both veneers where they overlap and the off-cuts are carefully removed by gently lifting the veneer. It may be necessary to apply a little heat to lift the veneer without it splitting. The veneer around the joint is then put down with the hammer, a little extra glue being applied if required When all the veneer is down all the joints between veneers should be covered with brown paper, laid over the joint in the same way as the veneer. Rolls of gummed brown paper are available for just this purpose If this is not done it will be found that the joint will open up during drying. The veneered surface must now be left for at least 24 hours to dry, then it can be cleaned up with the use of a cabinet scraper and

'The Pink Bonnet' in pearwood and walnut by Andrew
Smith of Wakefield would adorn any home.

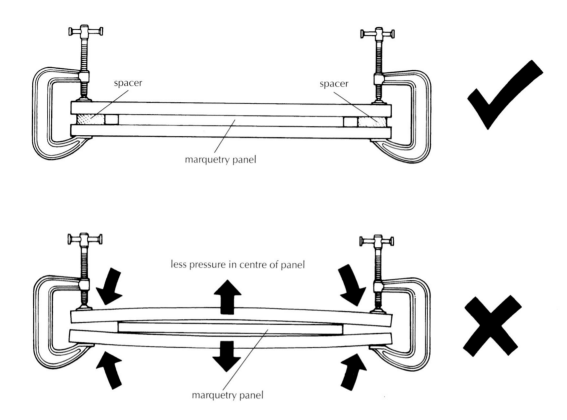

Fig 23 Spacer pieces prevent the press from bowing.

medium to fine sandpaper. Remember that you are dealing with a very thin piece of veneer: and be careful not to go through the surface when cleaning up. Any veneer which overhangs the edge can be cleaned off with a file or sharp chisel, remembering always to file or cut away from the veneer and towards the groundwork, to prevent splitting. It is a good idea to get some practice in putting some odd pieces of veneer down on some off-cuts of wood before tackling an important job. It is an easy matter to break or split the veneer with the veneering hammer if there is too much glue under the veneer, or if the glue is too thick, or was not hot enough.

If trouble is experienced and the glue starts to go off before the job is completed, then an ordinary household iron set to a medium temperature can be used to reheat the glue under the veneer. Be careful, however, not to have the iron too hot and ensure that there is plenty of glue on top of the veneer when using the hot iron to prevent burning.

CAUL METHOD

The caul method of laying veneer is the best method to use if several pieces of veneer are to be laid or if the veneer is saw-cut and is too thick to be laid with a hammer. The groundwork is prepared in the same way as for hammer laying. The caul or press itself is described on pages 16–17. If you are making the back quartered then the joints can be made beforehand and held in place with tape. Before applying any glue, the caul and all blocks that are to be used, as well as the cramps themselves, should be heated, the caul being made quite hot. Glue is spread over the surface to be veneered and allowed to cool enough so that it will not expand the veneer on contact. In fact it is possible to allow the glue to become quite cold, although this is not necessary. The veneer is then laid carefully in place and held in position with a couple of veneer pins. The caul is now placed over the work and cramped in place; the heat from the caul will penetrate through the veneer and remelt the glue. Pressure with the cramps should be applied from the middle outwards in order to squeeze out the excess glue.

COLD GLUE

When laying your veneer with cold glue it has to be kept under pressure until the glue is dry. On small panels this can be achieved by placing a flat board over the glued panel with a suitable weight on top; however, with most panels a press is to be recommended.

The glue should be applied evenly to the groundwork and left a few minutes for the excess moisture to evaporate. Place the picture onto the groundwork and press evenly over the surface to remove as much excess glue as possible, whilst ensuring that the mitres line up with the corners and all is in place. Clean off any glue that has squeezed out, and position in the press. If you are confident that the veneers are all the same thickness and that your groundwork is perfectly flat, then all you have to do is place a couple of sheets of newspaper over your picture and apply pressure with the press. The pressure must be applied a bit at a time starting with the centre cross-stretcher first, so that any remaining excess glue is squeezed out towards the edges.

If the panel in the press is very much smaller than the dimension of the press, it is important to put some spacer pieces of wood at the outer edges of the press, that are the same thickness as the groundwork and veneer. This has to be done under these circumstances to prevent the press from bowing in the middle when full pressure is applied.

FRAGMENTATION

Sometimes the marquetarian will come across an effect that he wants to portray – the autumn leaves on a tree, the pebbles on a beach, sweets in a jar – that cannot be achieved with a single veneer. These things can be successfully represented by fragmentation. Let us look at the problem of leaves on an autumn tree, as in 'New Hampshire Fall' by F. E. Kerridge, shown below and later.

The first step is to select the veneers to represent the various leaf colours, and with a straight edge, cut off strips about 1mm wide from each veneer. The strips are then chopped up so that a large quantity of

1mm-square bits of veneer are obtained and mixed together. A window, a little larger than that required for the actual picture, is then cut into a spare piece of veneer and the bottom of the window covered with masking tape. The window is placed on a flat hard surface, such as a piece of kitchen worktop, and is filled with PVA glue. The bits of veneer are sprinkled into the window and pressed flat, a piece of hardwood is held over the top and hammered down to expel all excess glue. Any excess glue from the surrounding area is wiped away, the window is then covered with a piece of polythene and the

Close-up of fragmentation used for the leaves in 'New Hampshire Fall' by F. E. Kerridge.

hardwood block cramped over the top until the glue is dry. Next day, the hardwood block and the polythene are removed and a check is made to ensure there are no hollow spots in the window, if there are then these are filled with more glue and fragments of veneer and cramped flat again. When dry, the fragments of veneer are sanded level with the surface of the waster, which can then be placed under the window proper in the picture and treated as a normal veneer.

SLIVERS

The slivers of veneer that you cut from the edge of a sheet in the first operation towards making the pieces for fragmentation can be used in a couple of other ways, instead of chopping them into small squares. When they are first cut, many of them will tend to curl up, and if one or two different colours are cut and then rolled together into a loose ball, and then pressed flat and glued into a waste window the same way as for fragmentation, a marbled effect can be achieved.

Alternatively the slivers can be straightened out and used for fine detail, such as the rigging on a ship, or the string of a

balloon. To use in this way, the window for the rigging or string is cut into the picture, keeping a regular thickness throughout its length, and the slivers are cut to the required thickness against a straight edge. A little glue is inserted into the window and the slivers are pressed into place using the end of a hammer.

TEMPLATES AND JIGS
TEMPLATE

When the picture requires that you cut a number of repeating components, such as roof tiles, cobblestones or even feathers, it is a good idea to make a cutting template. The template is best made from metal sheet, but thin hardwood can be used. Draw the item or items you have to cut onto some white paper and stick the paper onto the metal sheet or hardwood. Fretsaw out the required shape to leave a window. The template is used for the first score cut only, the veneer being transferred to the cutting mat for final cutting. Make sure that the sheet you are using for your template is large enough to be easily held in place over the veneer.

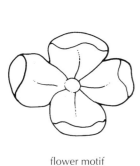

flower motif

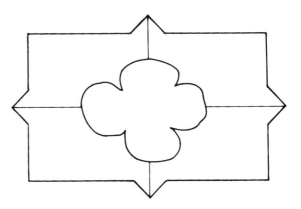

template for cutting outline of flower motif

Fig 24 Template.

JIG

The jig is basically a cutting mat that has stops on it so that a straight edge can be positioned to cut a desired angle or shape. Apart from the cutting jig for angles, there are three basic types of cutting jig for straight cuts, as follows.

Type A

This jig has a straight piece of wood or metal along one side against which the edge of the veneer can be held for cutting. To use, simply trim one edge of the veneer perfectly straight with a straight edge, hold this edge against the fence of the cutting jig, place a straight edge of the desired width on top of the veneer, also against the fence, and cut the veneer against this straight edge. The main disadvantage of this type of jig is the fact that the straight edge covers the veneer during cutting and there is no visual confirmation that the veneer is tight against the fence.

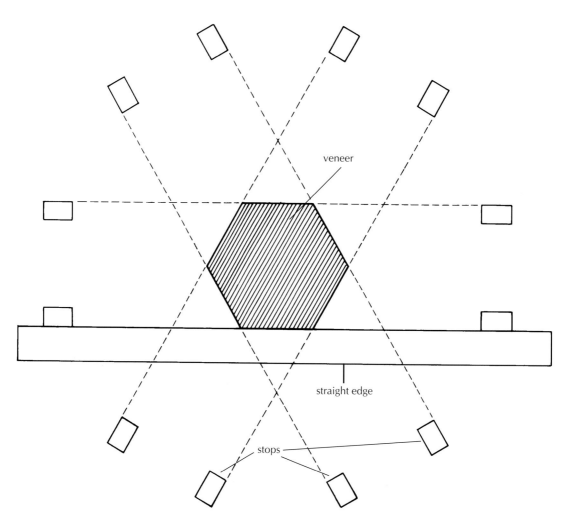

Fig 25 Jig for cutting hexagons.

Type B
This jig has the same basic table and the veneer is held against the fence in the same way as with jig A, but this time the straight edge is held against two stops pinned to the table of the jig. The advantage of this jig is that the veneer required can be seen to be against the fence during cutting. The disadvantage is that the blocks against which the straight edge is held need to be positioned very accurately.

Type C
This jig again has the same basic table as the other two, but the cutting itself is done with a cutting gauge held against the outer edge of the fence, rather than a knife. This is the most versatile of the three jigs shown.

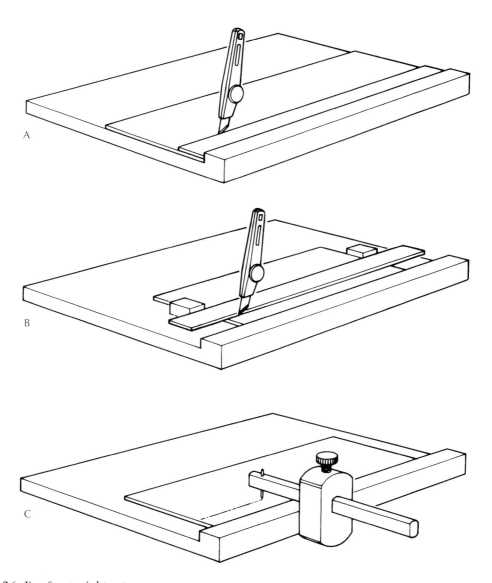

Fig 26 Jigs for straight cuts.

OTHER MATERIALS

TORTOISESHELL

Tortoiseshell is actually obtained from the shell of the marine turtle and can be cut from both the carapace that covers the animal's back and the plastron that protects its abdomen. The carapace is made up of thirteen plates, the plastron of either eighteen or twenty. The shell becomes pliable in hot water and solidifies under pressure. In antique marquetry, coloured paper was sometimes placed under the shell to enhance its colour.

HORN

The horn most commonly used in marquetry is cow horn, which is prepared for use in the following way. First the horn is cut into three sections: the throat, which is the part nearest the animal's skull, the biscage, which is tubular in shape and the tip that is conical. The throat is heated and then given a heavy blow with a bill hook to open it. The biscage is also heated, then cut one side and opened out in a spiral. The pieces are then flattened further by placing them in a heated press.

MOTHER-OF-PEARL

Mother-of-pearl is obtained from certain shells, of which trocas, a conical shell from the Philippines, Indonesia and Madagascar is the most common used. This mother-of-pearl is mainly white in colour. Mother of pearl with a greenish or sometimes bluish border is obtained from Ceylon, and some with a slightly greenish-black edge comes from California and Tahiti. Ear-of-the-sea and goldfish varieties with pinkish hues and spiral patterns come from the waters off Japan.

Mother-of-pearl is both hard and brittle and needs to be cut with a hand-held fretsaw rather than an electric one; and it is not advisable to try to cut more than two thicknesses at a time. The packet for cutting is made up in the usual way with the design glued to the top surface, as for wood veneer. After cutting, the packet can be placed in hot water for separation, and to remove the design.

SHAGREEN

Shagreen or sharkskin has been used since the early eighteenth century. It is light grey in colour but can be stained.

BONE

Cattle bone has a much whiter appearance than ivory. It is also harder, and more brittle to use. The bone is prepared for use by soaking for twelve days in a solution of 1250cl of water, 125g of sodium carbonate, and 20g of lime. The bone is then rinsed in water and then soaked in turpentine for 24 hours. After soaking in turpentine the bone is boiled in water for one hour. The bone can be bleached with hydrogen peroxide.

IVORY

For obvious reasons it is now very difficult to obtain ivory, unless one is lucky enough to find an old tusk in an auction or junk shop, but ivory substitutes that do not involve the killing of elephants can be purchased.

METALS

Brass is the most common metal used in marquetry and needs to be annealed to facilitate cutting. Silver, pewter and even gold, can, and have been used over the years. The fine detail is engraved onto the metal after the veneers have been laid.

F. E. Kerridge of South Cave in East Yorkshire made fine use of fragmentation in depicting the autumn leaves in 'New Hampshire Fall'.

PLASTIC

Various plastics such as celluloid have been around for some time now, and can be very useful; but when using these materials in conjunction with wood veneers, it is best if they are used slightly thinner than the wood, so that the cleaning-up stage is easier.

seven

PARQUETRY

Parquetry is the term used to describe marquetry patterns of a geometric nature. The patterns are used both as a decoration in their own right and as a background for marquetry patterns on furniture. Even greater accuracy is needed in the cutting of the various component parts, as any small difference in size or shape will show with a joint that is out of line, and any error will be compounded as the pattern progresses. For that reason the majority of the pieces required are cut on a jig with a straight edge; the measuring and marking out of the veneers themselves is largely avoided. When a strip of veneer is required to be a particular size, then a straight edge is made to the desired width and used against the side of the jig. The complexity and diversity of the patterns that can be made is endless, but the easiest to start with and the basis for many others is the chess board.

TOOLS

First, let us look at the additional tools that will be required, beyond those we have used for marquetry.

STRAIGHT EDGE

Most veneers in parquetry will be cut against a straight edge, and if, as is usually the case, you require several pieces that are exactly the same width, it is used in conjunction with the cutting jig shown in Fig 26.

SET SQUARES, PROTRACTOR AND A COMPASS

Instruments for marking out geometric patterns and drawing circles will be required for some parquetry patterns.

THE CUTTING JIG

These are explained in Chapter 6 Templates and Jigs.

THE CHESSBOARD

Let us assume that you have selected two contrasting coloured veneers of plain straight grain, such as mahogany and sycamore, for example, or sycamore and stained black, as used here to give a stark contrast. Decide what size you want the squares of your chessboard to be, and select or make a straight edge of this dimension. Prepare one edge of the veneer by cutting it straight against the straight edge. Place your veneer on the jig with the straight-cut edge against the fence and cut four strips of the one veneer and five of the other, ensuring that they are all exactly the same width. Tape or glue these strips together, and trim one end square with the straight edge, making sure that it is exactly at right-angles to the long joints. Return the assembled strips to the jig, this time placing the newly trimmed edge to the fence and cut off eight strips this time, each made up of alternating squares. Lay these strips on a flat surface and after carefully removing

The first cut.

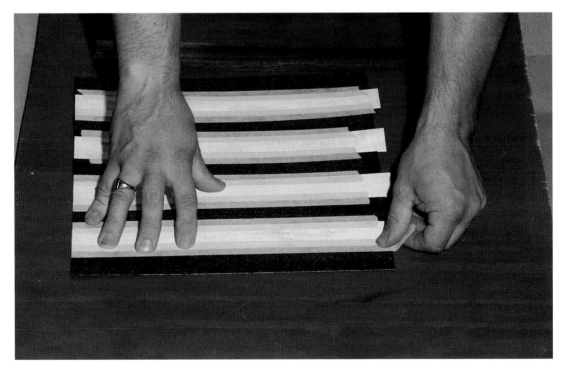

Tape the strips together.

Strips of alternating squares.

Move every other strip along one square.

Trim off the extra square.

the tape, move every other strip along one square, tape them together in this position and trim off the extra square. You should now have a perfect chessboard. You can now cut out your border and tape this around the edge of the chessboard prior to laying on the groundwork, just as you would for any marquetry picture.

In the method just described, the grain of all the squares, both mahogany and sycamore will be in the same direction, but you can, if you wish, cut one set of strips across the grain, so that when you tape the long strips together, you have one colour with long grain and one with cross-grain. This gives an extra contrast between the squares and also means that it is possible to make up a chequered pattern in this way using only one veneer, the contrast between the squares being purely that of grain direction.

ZIG-ZAGS AND TRIANGLES

The basic chessboard pattern can be used as the starting point to obtain some other designs. For instance, if you cut through the diagonals of one colour square, and move each of them along by half a square, you will have a zigzag pattern. If both veneers are cut though the diagonals and moved along you can obtain a double zigzag, and if alternate strips are then reversed, a pattern of alternate triangles is formed.

It can be seen that a variety of patterns can be easily obtained from moving the basic elements of a pattern of squares.

Some interesting patterns can also be made up of a basic diamond formation, either with the same two contrasting

The chessboard.

Cut through the diagonals.

The zig-zag.

Double zig-zag.

Triangle.

veneers as was used for the chessboard, or with strips of the same veneer, cut with the grain in different directions.

FIRST DESIGN: DIAMOND (FIG 27)

Cut a few strips of straight-grained veneer about 40mm wide with the grain parallel to the edges. Cut more strips of exactly the same width, but this time cut the strips at an angle of 60 degrees from the vertical. Tape or glue these strips together alternately, as shown. Now cut these veneers into strips across the ends at an angle of 60 degrees, corresponding to the grain direction of the second set of veneer strips, and slip every other strip along one space. You should now have a pattern of alternating diamonds, with the grains parallel to alternate sides.

SECOND DESIGN: DIAMOND (FIG 28)

The procedure for this is exactly the same as just described for the first design, except that the first strips are cut at an angle of 30 degrees to the vertical, rather than with the grain. The second strips are cut at 60 degrees as before, and they are taped or glued together alternately as with the first pattern. When this assembly is cut at 60 degrees and alternate strips slipped along, as was the previous one, it will reveal a pattern of diamonds with the grain alternately vertical and horizontal.

THIRD DESIGN

Proceed in the same way as for the second design, cutting the first strips at 30 degrees

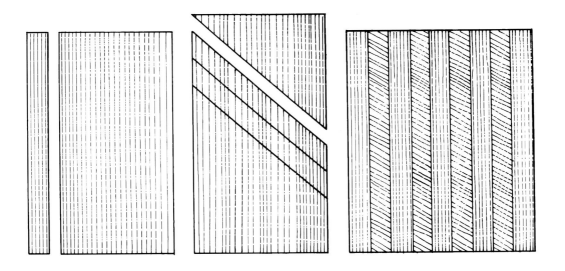

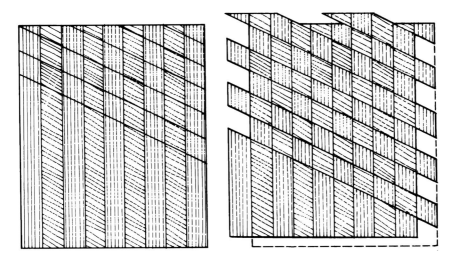

Fig 27 Cutting the diamond pattern.

and the second at 60 degrees to the grain. Tape them together as before, and cut cross-strips at 60 degrees. This time, instead of moving the strips along, cut again though the short diagonals of the diamonds and move these along one space. In this way a pattern of triangles is formed.

THE LOUIS CUBE

The Louis cube is formed by using the diamond shapes that we have been making in design one, with the grain parallel to two sides of the diamond. Three of these diamonds are assembled as a hexagon with the grain in different directions as shown on page 110. If you stare at the pattern, it is possible to see the interesting optical illusion, of being able to see cubes from either the top or the bottom. The ones shown are the background for an oval marquetry panel

TRELLIS

Trellis parquetry can be made up of squares, diamonds or even ovals and can be as simple or complex as you wish. The most usual design relies on a darkish background

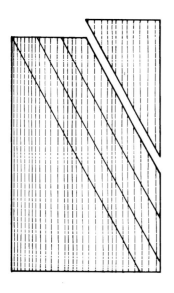
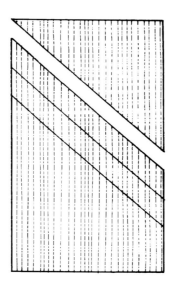

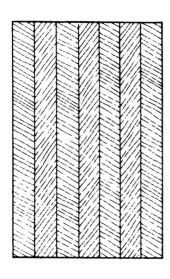
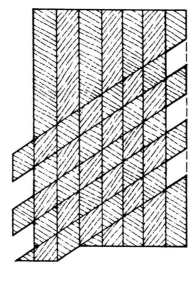

Fig 28 Second diamond pattern.

such as mahogany with light trellis-work of holly, sycamore or perhaps box. The straight strips of light veneer that are to be used for the trellis itself are cut on the cutting jig. The effect of the trellis interweaving is greatly enhanced if the ends of each piece of trellis are shaded in the sand box before assembly.

The background pieces, which are most commonly diamond in shape, can all be little pictures in themselves, with a flower, star or some other motif in the centre of

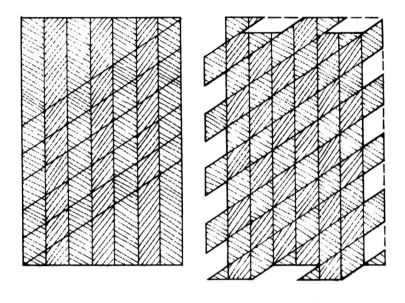

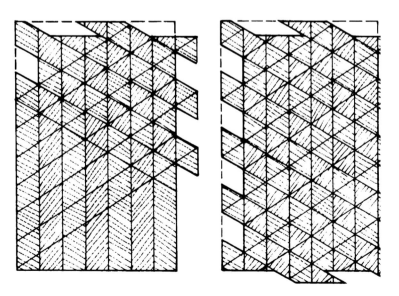

Fig 29 Triangles.

The Louis cube.

each. Remember that the background should look as if it is one piece, so continuity of grain is important, especially if there is no motif in the centre of the triangles or squares. When cutting the squares or diamonds for the trellis background, be sure to keep the pieces in order for assembly. If motifs are to be used between the trellis, you might consider making a stamp rather like a shaped pastry cutter, with which to stamp out the motifs. Alternatively you might like to make a template, or make up a pack of veneers to be cut with a fretsaw.

GEOMETRY

When producing parquetry designs or making panels other than the usual rectangle, it will be necessary to know a little basic geometry, in order to be able to draw triangles, pentagons, hexagons, etc.

Some definitions:
- A point is that which has position, but no dimension, neither length, breadth, nor thickness.
- A line is length, without breadth or thickness. The extremities of a line are points, and when two lines cross each

Fig 30 Trellises.

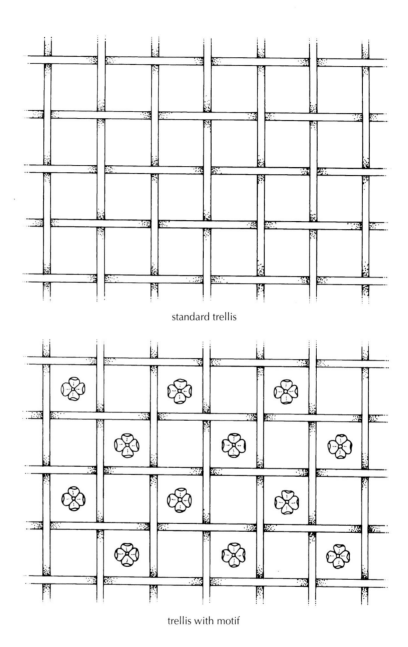

standard trellis

trellis with motif

other, their intersection is a point.
- A surface is a figure of two dimensions, length and breadth but without thickness. The space contained within the surface is called the area.
- A body or solid is a figure of three dimensions: length, breadth and depth or thickness.

- A circle is a plane figure bounded by one curved line, called the circumference, that is always equally distant from a point within it called the centre.
- A radius of a circle is a straight line drawn from the centre to the circumference.
- A diameter of a circle is a line drawn

'Lilies' by Pauline Stevens, wife of Eddy who also features here with 'In a Position to Know', was on show at the 44th National Marquetry Exhibition in Winchester.

through the centre and terminating at the circumference at both ends.

- A circle is divided into 360 degrees, 90 degrees being a right-angle.
- Plane figures bounded by straight lines have names according to the number of their sides, for they have the same number of angles as sides.
- Three is the least number of straight lines by which a space can be circumscribed, and as this figure has three angles it is called a triangle:

> an equilateral triangle has all its sides equal;
> an isosceles triangle has two of its angles equal;
> a triangle that has all its sides unequal is called a scalene triangle;
> a right-angled triangle has one of its angles a right-angle;
> an obtuse angled triangle has one of its angles greater than 90 degrees;
> an acute angled triangle has all of its angles less than 90 degrees.

- Figures having four sides and angles are known as quadrangles and receive different denominations according to the relation of those sides and angles.
- A parallelogram is a quadrangle which has both its pairs of sides parallel, and it has six types:

> the rectangle is a parallelogram all the angles, of which are right-angles;
> the square is a parallelogram that has all its angles right-angles and all its sides equal;
> a rhomboid is a parallelogram that has all its angles oblique and opposite pairs of sides are unequal in length;
> a rhombus is an equilateral rhomboid having all its sides equal but its angle oblique. This figure is also known as a lozenge;
> a trapezoid has only one pair of oppsite sides parallel;
> a trapezium has no sides parallel.

- Plane figures having more than four sides are called polygons. They receive other names according to their number of sides or angles. A pentagon has five sides, a hexagon six, a heptagon seven, an octagon eight, a nonagon nine, a decagon ten, an undecagon eleven and a dodecagon twelve. Polygons that have more than twelve sides are generally designated by the number of their sides.

A polygon is regular when it has its sides and angles equal, and irregular if its sides or angles are unequal; it is the regular figures that interest us most in parquetry, as these can be built up to form larger and more intricate shapes.

SOME BASIC PROBLEMS
TO BISECT A LINE AT RIGHT-ANGLES

Draw a line AB, place a compass point on one end of the line and open the compasses so that the pencil is well past the half-way mark. Scribe an arc above and below the line, at C and D and repeat with the compass point on the other end of the line, draw a line connecting the two points where the arcs crossed, and this line will bisect the line A B in the centre and at right-angles.

TO DRAW A PENTAGON WITHIN A CIRCLE

Scribe a circle the desired size around the point X and draw in the diameter AC, bisect this diameter as just described and draw in the diameter BD. Bisect the radius AX and from E with the radius EB scribe an arc to meet AC at F. The distance BF is the chord of the fifth part of the circumference. Place the compass point on B with the radius BF and mark the circumference at G and H, place the compass point on G to mark I and on H to mark J. Join these marks to form the pentagon.

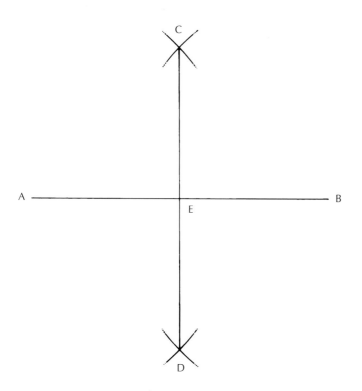

Fig 31 To bisect a line at right-angles.

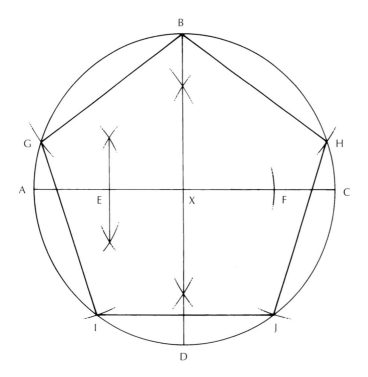

Fig 32 To draw a pentagon within a circle.

TO DRAW A PENTAGON HAVING SIDES OF A GIVEN LENGTH

Draw the first side the desired length A B, raise a line BC perpendicular to it at B and equal to half the length AB. Draw a line from A through C and extend it beyond C until CD is equal to CB. Scribe arcs from A and B with the radius equal to the distance BD so that they intersect at E. From E with the radius EA or EB scribe a circle. With the compasses open to the distance AB place the point on B and mark the circumference at F, put the point on A and mark H and finally with the point on F or H, mark G. Join these marks together to form the pentagon.

TO DRAW A REGULAR POLYGON OF ANY NUMBER OF SIDES OF A GIVEN LENGTH

Let AB be the given line of the required length. Extend AB at least as far again and

Angles for creating a polygon	
Number of sides	Angle at centre
3	120 degrees
4	90 degrees
5	72 degrees
6	60 degrees
7	51⅜ degrees
8	45 degrees
9	40 degrees
10	36 degrees
11	32⁸⁄₁₁ degrees
12	30 degrees

with B as the centre describe a semi-circle with the radius BA. The semi-circle is divided into the given number of sides required – five for a pentagon, six for a hexagon, etc. Draw a line from B to the second division and make this line equal to AB. These two lines, AB and BD, are the first two lines of the polygon. Bisect these two lines at E and F so that they intersect at

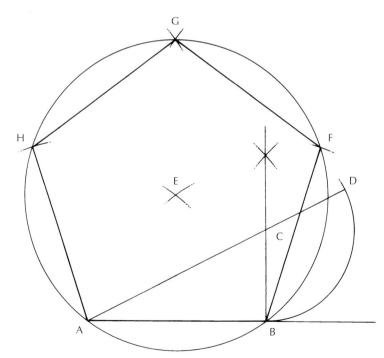

Fig 33 To draw a pentagon having sides of a given length.

115

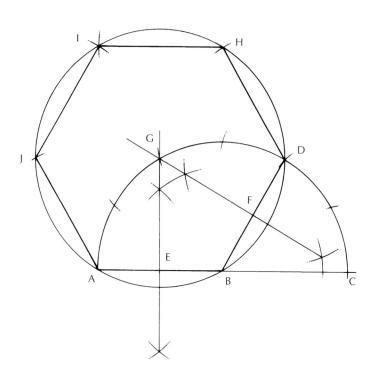

G. With G as the centre, describe a circle with the radius GB. With the radius AB, scribe arcs from D to H and so on round the circle. Join these arcs to produce the required polygon.

The principle of the construction is that the exterior angle of the polygon at DBC is equal to the angle at the centre, and a protractor can be used by referring to the table on the previous page.

TO DRAW AN ELLIPSE

There will come a time when it will be necessary to draw an ellipse, either for some parquetry design, or because the marquetry picture is to be mounted in an oval panel, something that is often seen on pieces of furniture. Whatever the reason, it may be of interest to know something about this most interesting of shapes.

An ellipse is the figure that is formed by the intersection of a cone, by a plane that

cuts both the slanting sides in any direction not parallel to the base, for if the section was parallel to the base, then the section would be a circle. The other conic sections are the parabola, which is formed by the intersection of the cone by a plane that is parallel to one of the sides, and the hyperbola, which is any other section that does not cut both sides.

The outer line of the ellipse is the circumference; any line drawn through the centre of the ellipse and meeting the circumference both ways is known as a diameter. However, unlike the circle, where all diameters are the same length, each diameter of an ellipse has only one other that is equal to it. The longest diameter is known as the transverse axis, AB, and the shortest as the conjugate axis, CD. These two axes are often referred to as the major and minor axes.

Two points of great importance lie on the major or transverse axis of the ellipses, and these points, F and G, are known as the foci of the ellipse. The foci are so situated that if a line is drawn to each from any point on the circumference, the sum of the two lines will always be equal to the greater diameter, or major axis. This fact means that it is easy to determine the position of these two points in the following way.

First, draw the major axis, AB. Place a compass point on A and open the compass so that the distance between point and pencil is greater than half of the major axis, and scribe an arc, H, on the axis. Place the point of the compass on B and do the

same, scribing the arc I. Now place the compass point on H and I in turn and scribe arcs above and below the major axis at points J and K. If a line is drawn from I to J it will bisect the major axis in the centre E and the minor axis can be drawn. Open the compass to the radius AE or EB, place the point on C and scribe an arc cutting the major axis at points JJ. Points JJ are the foci of the ellipse.

To draw an ellipse first draw the major and minor axes and locate the foci as just

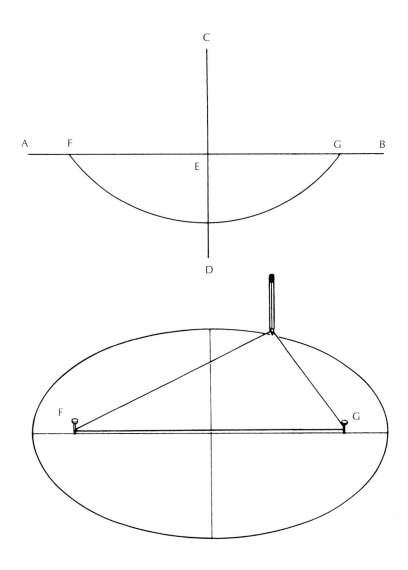

Fig 35 Transverse and conjugate axis.

Fig 36 Second method of drawing an ellipse.

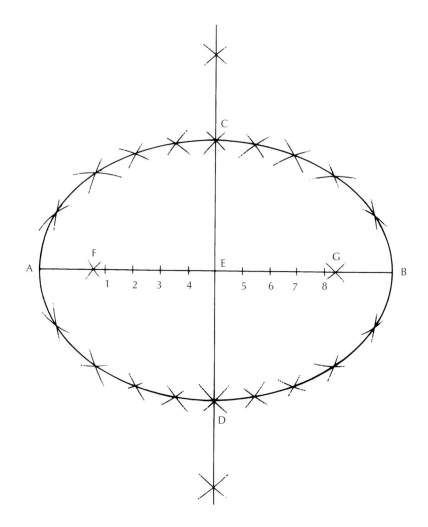

described. Place pins at the foci points JJ, loop the centre of a piece of string around the end of a pencil and place the pencil point on either C or D. Pull the string taut and tie the ends off on the pins at JJ. Keeping the string taut at all times, the circumference of the ellipse can be drawn.

SECOND METHOD

First the major and minor axes are drawn, as for the first method, and the foci of the ellipse are located by scribing an arc from C with the diameter AE. The major axis is now divided into a number of equal parts. The greater the number of divisions, the easier it is to draw the ellipse. Now with the foci as centres a number of arcs are scribed, with the diameters G1, G2, G3, etc., and then F8, F7, F6, and so on. These arcs will cross on the circumference of the ellipse, so the circumference can be drawn by joining these points together.

COMPOSITION

If you are copying an existing picture in its entirety, then all the relevant details of construction and composition will have been worked out for you, but if you are making your own picture from scratch, or copying from real life, then decisions have to be taken to determining the shape and proportions of the picture. Pictures can be either square, portrait, or landscape in shape; portrait simply means that it is taller than it is wide, and landscape means wider than it is tall. The proportion of height to width will largely depend upon the subject matter. Truly square pictures are rare, and one rule of thumb is to make a landscape picture half as wide again as it is tall and portrait pictures half as tall again as they are wide. Some artists will say that there is a perfect proportion and that this is obtained by selecting the most important measurement for either the base or side of the picture and multiply it by 0.618 for a smaller dimension or 1.618 for a larger dimension. This would mean for instance that if it has been decided that the base of a landscape picture should be 25cm, then multiplying 25cm by 0.168 will give 15.45cm as the ideal height.

PERSPECTIVE

Perspective is basically the means by which an impression of three dimensions is produced on a two-dimensional plane, and some understanding of this topic is necessary if realistic pictures are to be produced.

The first thing to be determined is the position of the horizon. With portrait pictures it is usual to position the horizon the same distance as the width of the picture from either the top or bottom. With landscape pictures it can be placed approximately a third of the way up from the bottom or down from the top, or it is possible to multiply the height by 0.618 and position the horizon this distance from either the top or bottom of your picture. Whatever method you use for selecting the position of the horizon, always remember that you need one, even for portraits and interior scenes, although in those instances it is less confusing if we refer to the eye-level rather than the horizon.

Once the horizon or eye-level has been drawn, at least one vanishing point will be required. This is the point or points where all parallel lines that are not parallel to the observer converge or disappear on the horizon. Lines that are parallel to the observer, that is to say vertical and horizontal lines that cross the picture parallel to the observer remain parallel, but get closer together the further away they are. The usual example used to illustrate this is of railway lines viewed from the centre with telegraph poles running along one side. The sides of the railway line converge at the vanishing point on the horizon, but the railway sleepers and the telegraph poles remain parallel but get closer together until they appear to join. However because most objects are not viewed square on, it will normally be necessary to have at least two vanishing points, and often several.

Figure 38 shows how the outline of a barn is drawn in perspective, using two vanishing points. The first ground line of the

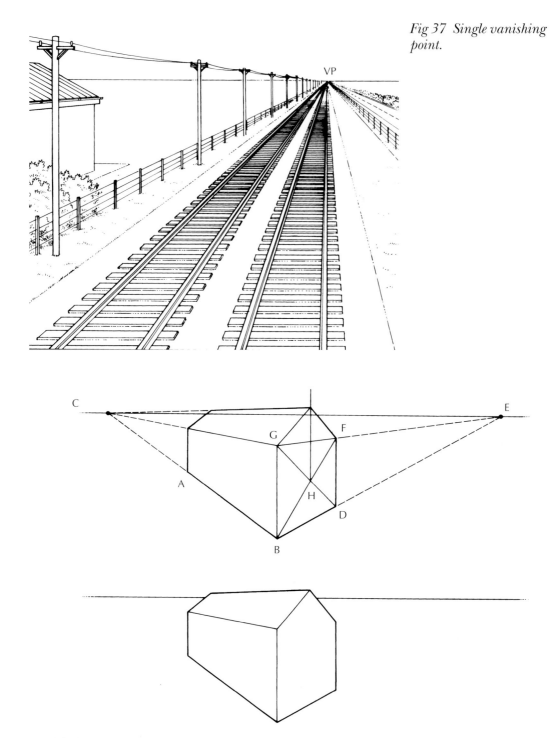

Fig 37 Single vanishing point.

Fig 38 Outline of a barn drawn in perspective.

Eddy Stevens got his idea for 'In a Position to Know' from the 'Fadeaway Girls' of Coles Phillips, 1880–1927.

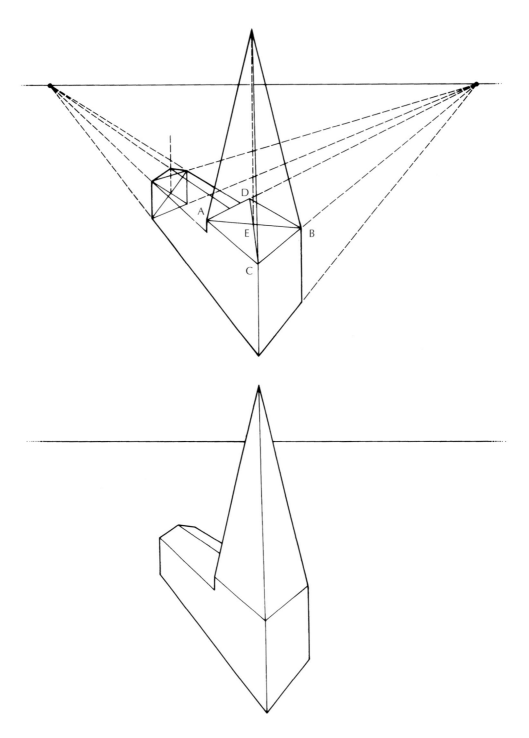

Fig 39 Locating the centre of a spire.

barn AB is drawn in and is continued to the vanishing point C on the horizon. The second ground line DB is drawn, and this is continued to the vanishing point E. Points C and E are now the two vanishing points on the horizon for all lines parallel to those just drawn. That is to say that all lines parallel to the left side of the barn converge at point C, whereas all parallel lines to the front of the barn vanish at point E. All vertical lines remain vertical. If another building is drawn, facing the same way as the barn, so that the sides of one are parallel with the other, then the same two vanishing points are used; however, if the other building is located at an angle to the barn, new vanishing points will be needed. The first two ground lines are drawn in place as for the first barn, and continued to the horizon where they will become new vanishing points for all new lines that are parallel with them.

The apex of the roof is located by first finding the true perspective centre of the front and rear of the building, as this is not the centre of the distance between the two walls. In order to find the perspective centre a cross is drawn between the corners DG and BF and the centre is located where these lines cross. A vertical line is drawn up from the intersection of the cross and the apex of the roof will be located somewhere

on this line depending on the slope of the roof. This technique is also employed to locate the centre of such things as church spires, as can be seen from Fig 39. The main body of the building is drawn in the same way as the barn. Although the church is being viewed from a higher point the same principles apply. The centre of the square base of the spire is located by joining the corners A, B and C, and D, drawing a perpendicular line up from the intersection E. The centre of the spire can be located at any point on this line, depending on the height.

CONVERGENCE

It has already been stated that parallel lines that are parallel to the observer, either vertical or horizontal, remain parallel, but that they appear to get closer together or converge, the further away they are. The following technique is used for determining the reducing distance between receding objects such as fence posts, railway sleepers and the like. First the eye level is drawn and then the post AB nearest to the observer. A line is then drawn from the top and bottom of this post to a vanishing point on the horizon. The second post CD is drawn a suitable distance from the first and its height is restricted to the distance

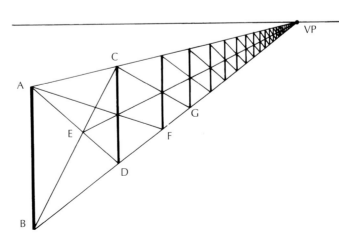

Fig 40 Receding posts.

between the two lines AVP and BVP. Now the centre point of the rectangle ABCD is determined by drawing in the diagonals. A further line is then drawn from the point where the diagonals meet at e to the vanishing point (VP). A line is now drawn from the top of the first post at A through the point where the line from E intersects the second post and is continued until it reaches the line from B to VP at F. The point F is the position of the third post. Draw a new line from C through the point where EVP intersects the third post and continue it to G, the position of the fourth post, and so on.

TO DIVIDE A GIVEN SPACE INTO THE REQUIRED NUMBER OF SECTIONS

Let us now look at the problem of the fence post again, but this time there are eight posts and they have to be placed along the

side of a field or road that is a given length. First of all, the side of the field AB is drawn and this line is continued to the vanishing point on the horizon. The first post AC is drawn the required height, and a line drawn from the top of this post to the vanishing point, and this allows the far end post to be drawn in perspective at the other end of the field at BD. There are now six more posts to be placed at regular intervals between A and B. A ground line is drawn, EF, and the line of the first post AC extended to meet the horizon at G and the newly drawn ground line at E. A line is drawn from G through the base of the far post at B and continued until it meets the ground line at F. The ground line EF is now divided into the required number of divisions – in this case seven, to correspond with the number of spaces between posts. These divisions are now linked to the point G and the points where they intersect the line AB are the positions of the posts.

Although the example used here to demonstrate the principle involved was posts at the side of a field, the posts could just as easily have been the sides of windows

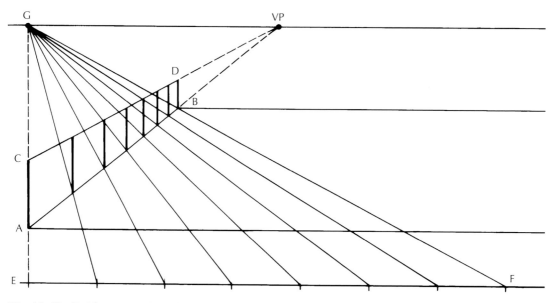

Fig 41 To divide a space into the required number of sections.

in a house, the blocks in a wall or the sides of houses in a street. The principle remains the same.

THE SQUARE
(ONE-POINT PERSPECTIVE)

The simplest way to draw a perfect square in one-point perspective is to position two more vanishing points equidistant either side of the central vanishing point. The observer is positioned centrally by dropping a line from the central VP. The base of the square is drawn in the desired width and lines drawn from the ends of the base line to the central VP. Other lines are now drawn from the ends of the base line to the two outer vanishing points. The other base line is draw between the points where the diagonals cross the lines from the central VP. Figure 43 shows how a cube is constructed using this method. The base line

is drawn AB and the bottom of the cube constructed as was the square. Verticals are then drawn up from A and B with the same dimension as AB and the tops of these verticals connected to form the top of the front edge of the cube CD. Lines are then taken from CD to the vanishing point and the back verticals brought up to meet them at EF.

THE SQUARE
(TWO-POINT PERSPECTIVE)

Drawing a square in two-point perspective is slightly more difficult than in one-point, because all sides recede and are therefore foreshortened. In many instances it will be possible to estimate the proportions of squares and rectangles, but if more precision is needed, then plan projection can be used as follows. First the square is drawn in plan and the position of the

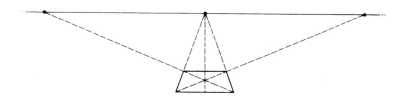

Fig 42 The square in one-point perspective.

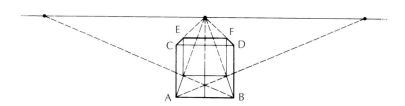

Fig 43 The cube in one-point perspective.

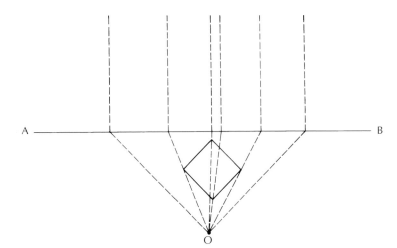

Fig 44 The square is first drawn in plan.

observer determined O. Lines are drawn from O exactly parallel to the sides of the square and extending to a line AB that represents the base of the picture plane. The distance of the picture plane from the plan controls the scale of the drawing. Lines are projected from O through the four corners of the plan square, and one directly vertical through the central line of vision to the picture plane. From their point of intersection with the picture plane all lines are extended vertically to

the chosen eye-level at VP1, VP2 and CV1. The point of the near corner of the square is marked on the projected line at an appropriate position below eye-level, and when this point is connected to the vanishing points the method of construction becomes clear. It is also possible to construct a cube using this method by including a height line in the projections. One side of the plan square is projected to the picture plane where it is then extended vertically to the eye level. A ground line is

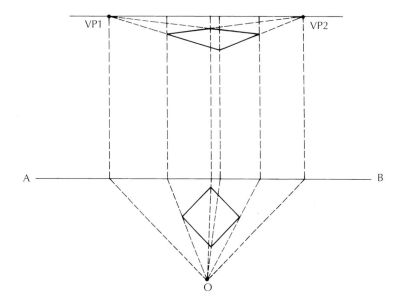

Fig 45 Drawing the square in perspective.

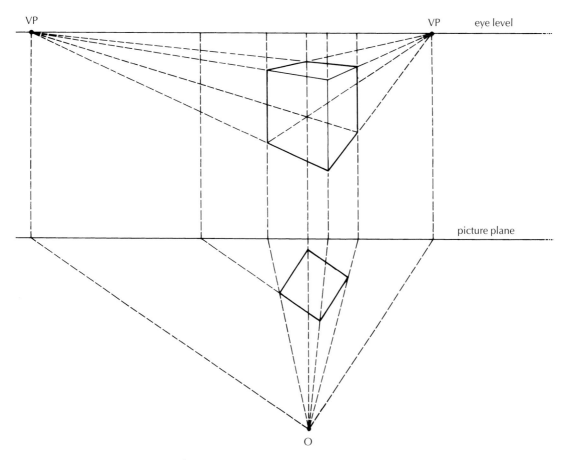

Fig 46 Constructing a cube from the plan.

drawn in an appropriate place below eye-level. To establish the position of the near corner a line is projected from the left vanishing point through the point of intersection of the height line and ground line to where it meets the near corner projection. The base of the cube is constructed as was the square, and then a point marked on the height line by measuring up from its intersection with the ground line to a point equal to the dimension of one of the sides of the plan square. A line is then projected from the left VP through this new point to intersect with the near corner projection, and this is then the height of the front edge.

THE CUBE IN THREE-POINT PERSPECTIVE

Shown in Fig 47 is a cube drawn in three-point perspective, first using the eye-level for the first two vanishing points, and then using a slanting line instead of the natural eye level to show the cube tilted both towards the observer and to the right.

THE CIRCLE

When a circle is drawn in perspective it becomes an ellipse, and because a circle can be fitted inside a square, one of the best ways to draw the perspective circle is to draw it

127

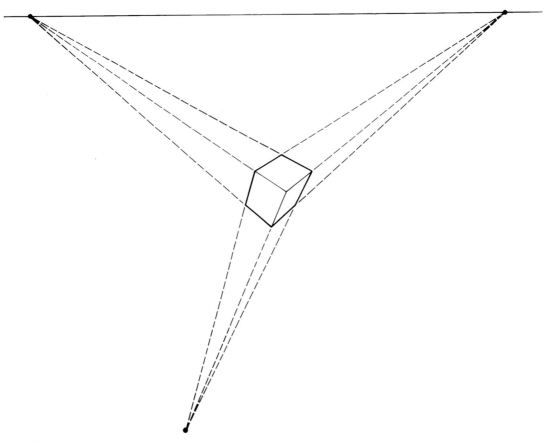

Fig 47 Three-point perspective.

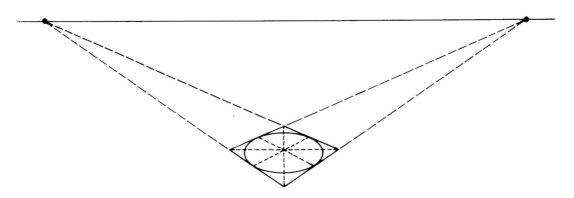

Fig 48 The circle in perspective.

within the confines of a perspective square. The square in Fig 48 was drawn using the method illustrated in Fig 45, and it was then subdivided as shown. One effect that can be seen is that the widest part of the ellipse is in front of the natural centre of the circle.

STAIRS

Flights of stairs are often seen in marquetry pictures, and their construction in one-point perspective can be clearly seen in Fig 49. First the eye-level and the centre line of vision are drawn in. The length and height of the first step is drawn in as a rectangle and the inclined plane of the stairs is governed by the positioning of the vanishing point at B. The four corners of the first riser are projected to B to give the widths

of all other risers and the first tread is drawn by projecting lines from the top of the first riser, back towards the central VP at A until the intersect with the projected lines from the bottom of the first riser. A vertical line is drawn up from this point to intersect the top line and the process repeated to the desired height.

The construction of stairs in two-point perspective should now be clear (*see* Fig 50).

REFLECTIONS

Many marquetry pictures involve water and reflected images, and it may be helpful here to give an example of a reflected image, as contrary to what may be thought at first, what is seen reflected is not what is

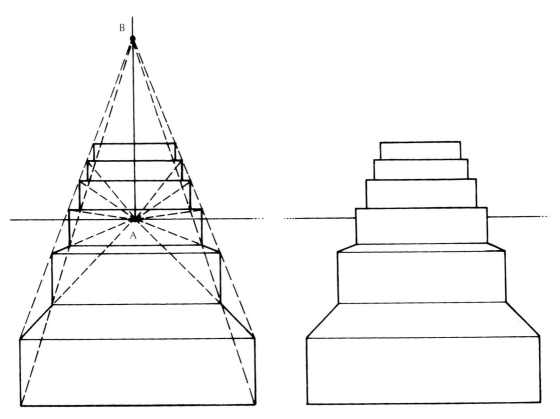

Fig 49 Stairs in one-point perspective.

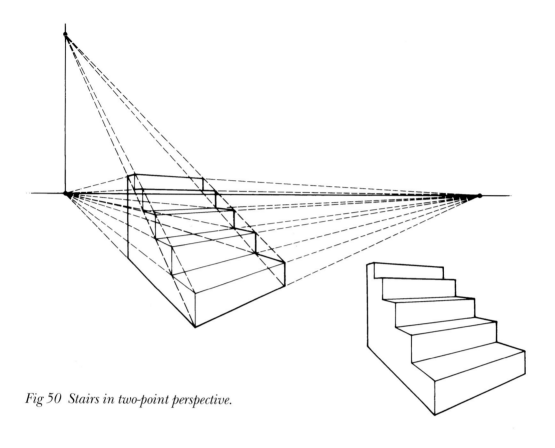

Fig 50 Stairs in two-point perspective.

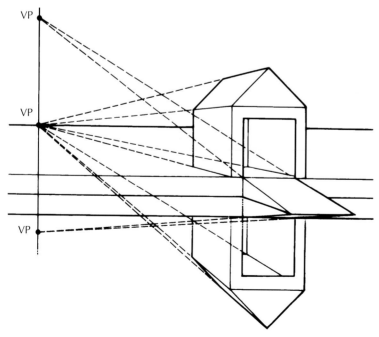

Fig 51 The boathouse is reflected in the water.

seen in the original, and this discrepancy is due to perspective.

Let's take a simple example of a boathouse on the edge of a river bank drawn in one-point perspective. The horizon or eye-level is established and the riverbank itself drawn in together with the reflection of the riverbank. The front of the boathouse is drawn square-on, but the sides converge at the vanishing point on the horizon, as does the top of the roof line. The launching ramp slopes to the water and its sides converge at a second vanishing point, which because the sides are parallel to the sides of the boathouse is located directly above the first vanishing point. It is helpful at first to draw the boathouse as if it were made of glass, so that the floor and interior wall can be correctly located. The reflection of the front of the boathouse is drawn in lightly. Now the reflections of the sides are drawn in, and this is where things begin to show a difference between original and reflection. The reflected sides converge on the same vanishing point as the original, but the angle will be different because the reflection is further away from the eye-level or horizon, and thus in the reflection the ceiling inside the boathouse is visible and the floor cannot be seen at all. To establish a vanishing point for the reflection of the launching ramp a line is drawn down from the first and a point measured an equal distance below from the horizon as the original is up above it.

SHADOWS

When drawing shadows in perspective, we require the assistance of two new vanishing points, one being the vanishing point of light and the other being the vanishing point of shadow. The vanishing point of light is always located at the light source itself, whereas the location of the vanishing point of shadow differs, depending on whether the light is coming from sunlight or an artificial source. If the light is coming from the sun, the vanishing point of shadow is located directly below the sun on the horizon or eye level, whereas if the light source is artificial in origin then the vanishing point of shadow is located directly below the light source on the ground rather than the eye-level. The reason for this difference in location is because the sun is so far away from the earth that light rays fall to earth virtually parallel.

In the example shown for the sun, lines were projected from the sun through the near upper corners of the cube to an approximate position on the ground, and one line dropped down to the eye-level to provide the vanishing point of shadow. Lines were then projected from the vanishing point of shadow through the bottom corners of the cube to intersect the lines from the sun. Linking the points of intersection formed the outline of the shadow.

In the example just detailed the sun was in front of the observer, casting a shadow to the front of the cube, but often the sun will be deemed to be behind the observer; the solution to this is shown in Fig 53. The cube is drawn in exactly the same way as with the sun in view. A position for the sun is established on the drawing surface the same distance below the eye-level as the sun is deemed to be above it, S1. The sun position S1 is then projected across to a position an equal distance the other side of the centre of vision, S2. Lines are then projected to the upper corners of the cube and a vertical taken up to the eye level to give the vanishing point of shadow. Again the points of intersection from S2 and vanishing points are joined to give the outline of the shadow.

Looking at the cube in Fig 54 will show you the difference with an artificial light source. All is the same except the positioning of the vanishing point of shadow which is now located at a point on the ground directly below the light source.

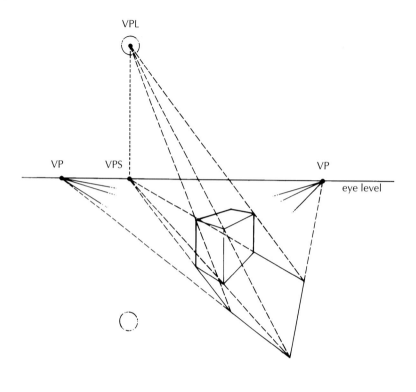

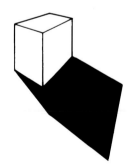

Fig 52 Shadow cast by the sun.

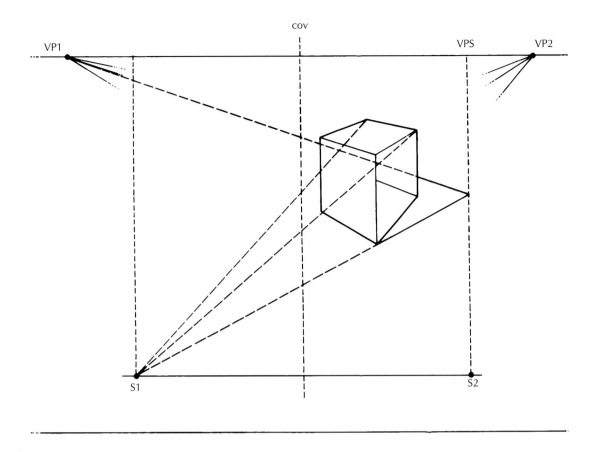

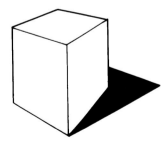

Fig 53 Shadow cast when the sun is behind the observer.

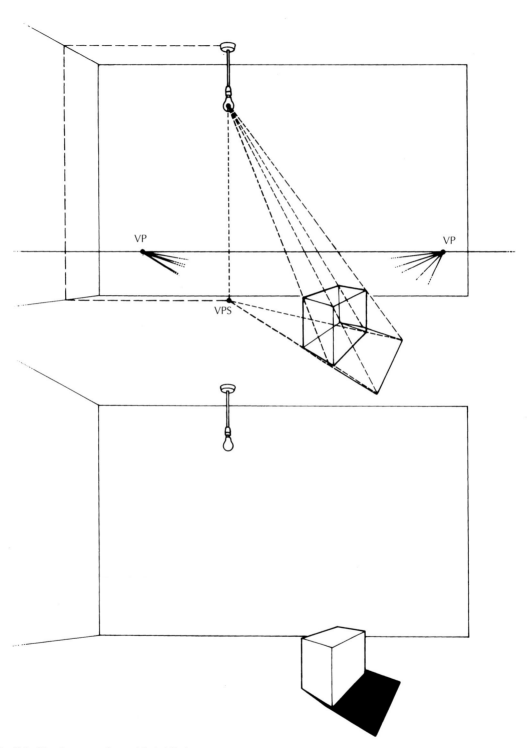

Fig 54 Shadow cast by artificial light.

PREPARATION FOR FINISHING

When the finished picture is removed from the cramps, it is best if it is left for a couple of days for the glue to harden fully and for the veneers to adjust to the temperature and humidity of their surroundings. The picture will then have to be scraped and sanded, as a prelude to the finishing process. This is done both to make sure that all the veneers are flat and level, and to ensure that all traces of adhesive are removed from the top surface. The first sanding can be carried out with a medium-grade paper and further sandings with progressively finer grades.

Before applying the first finishing coat It is a good idea to wet the surface with methylated spirit, as this will help to show up any remaining adhesive or other blemish that is difficult to see when the veneers are dry. When the picture is ready for the finishing process it must be ensured that the surface is dust-free This is best achieved by going over the surface with a vacuum cleaner.

METHODS OF FINISHING

WAX POLISHING

If we have decided to use a wax finish then first we have to make up some suitable wax to use. Shred some beeswax into a bowl with a little turpentine. Place the bowl in a saucepan of hot water and stir until the beeswax has dissolved, then add a little copal varnish to harden it when it cools. Do not have the wax so hard that it is difficult

to apply. It is better to have it soft and leave it to stand for a few hours before buffing up. Apply the wax with a soft cloth, allow an hour or so for it to harden and buff it up with a clean rag. It will be necessary to repeat the operation several times to obtain a good result and it will involve a great deal of elbow grease.

A Quick Method
Alternatively you could apply two coats of shellac or one of sanding sealer with a polishing mop. This must be done with the grain and allowed to dry for about half an hour before being rubbed down with either fine steel wool or flour paper between coats. After the last coat has dried it must again be rubbed down lightly and then waxed. The application of a couple of coats of shellac before waxing means that much of the grain will be filled and less wax and less hard work will be needed. There are many preparatory waxes on the market but many of them will be coloured and therefore unsuitable for marquetry. Make sure they are colourless, have a beeswax base and are free of silicon.

FRENCH POLISHING

French polishing is a method of applying shellac diluted with methylated spirits. French polish is applied with a pad, or rubber, which is a wad of cotton wool covered with a clean cotton rag, and a very high gloss can be obtained. French polish itself is quite brown in colour and will impart this to your picture. This is fine if

Make a cotton wool pad.

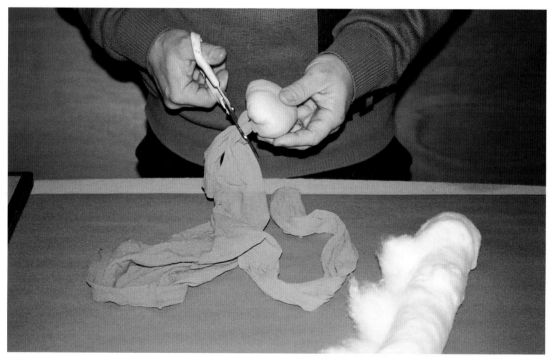

A stocking leg helps to keep the pad in shape.

Use clean cotton rag.

Remove the rag when replenishing the pad.

you are looking for an antique appearance to your work, but not so good in other cases. To overcome the problem of colour it is possible to purchase 'white polish' which is produced in exactly the same way, except that the shellac has been bleached, and consequently will not colour your work.

To make a pad, you take some cotton wool and shape it to fit in the hand comfortably with the fingers wrapped around the sides. How large a piece will depend on the size of the job. Place the shaped cotton wool inside a stocking leg and tie it off, cutting off the excess. This will help it to keep its shape and prevent bits of wool escaping and getting onto the work. Cover the whole thing in a piece of clean washed cotton rag – an old, washed handkerchief is ideal. Always remove the rag when charging the pad with polish.

The process of French polishing can be divided into three stages.

Stage One (Fadding)

The polish is used fairly thickly. The idea is to get as much polish as possible onto the work surface. This process is known as fadding and is done with a fad, which is a pad or rubber with only a very coarse cover. The polish is applied by rubbing the pad over the surface in figure-of-eight movements, both lengthwise and across the panel. Make sure that you get plenty of polish on the edges and into the corners of your panel; the centre will build up naturally but corners are easily neglected. The panel should then be left overnight to harden off, and sanded down with fine flour paper before polishing recommences.

Stage Two

To start, the pad is filled with polish which has been thinned with methylated spirit to about two parts polish to three parts methylated spirits. It should be filled so that when it is squeezed lightly polish oozes through the cotton rag. The pad is then wiped over the surface to be polished, first in the direction of the grain, leaving a thin film of polish behind. At first when the pad is very wet a lot of polish will be squeezed out and care must be taken not to go over the same area again until the polish is seen to dry, but gradually as the pad dries you will find that you can go back over an area almost at once without the pad sticking. This is when you must go over the job in as many directions as possible, using circular and figure-of-eight movements, and keep working in this way until the pad is dry. The pad can be refilled several times and the idea at this stage is to get as much polish as possible onto the surface without the pad sticking. The polish must now be left overnight to harden and then it can be rubbed down with flour paper or fine steel wool and the process repeated, but this time with slightly more dilute polish. The pad can then be kept in an airtight container when not in use.

This process must be continued until the grain of the wood is filled completely. You will find that the grain in the middle of your job will fill more quickly than the edges and corners, so it is a good idea to try and concentrate your efforts on the outside edges and make sure you get right into those corners. The biggest danger you will encounter when polishing in this way is burning the polish. This is where you go over an area before the polish has had a chance to dry. This is usually because you have put the pad down a little hard on the job and too much polish has come out and consequently taken longer to dry. When you go over this wet area of polish, instead of leaving more polish on a job, you are more likely to take off that which is already there. When this happens you must not try to build it up again right away, which will only result in failure, with even more polish being removed. You must leave the job

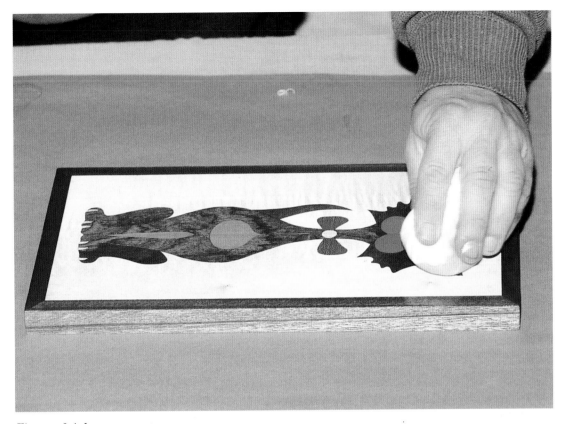

Figure-of-eight movement.

overnight until it can be rubbed down. The other thing that can cause burning is polish getting sticky on the edge of your pad, so always make sure that you have a clean pad and if the pad feels at all sticky change to a clean area of rag. It is possible to make life a little easier when polishing by lubricating the surface with a little polishing oil. This is used by smearing a small amount onto the palm of the hand and then wiping the edge of the pad in it. Use the oil sparingly, because it leaves a film on the job which has to be removed later. As you gain more experience with polishing you will use less oil.

After the work has been left overnight, it can be rubbed down with fine flower paper or 0000 wire wool and the process repeated. As the work progresses use ever more dilute polish, ending up with polish which is more spirit than shellac.

Stage Three

The third stage comes when the grain is completely filled and this is called 'spiriting off'. Make a completely new pad and instead of filling it with polish, put just a few drops of methylated spirit onto the cotton wool and cover with a clean rag, then place the pad into an airtight container until the spirit has permeated right through the pad. The pad is then used in the same way as before and this will gradually remove the oil from the surface and impart that extra little shine. If, when you rub a finger over the surface of the job, it leaves a trace, then you know that there is still some oil on the surface. When all of the oil is gone, your job is complete.

Do not expect to obtain a perfect result first time. Remember the pad must be kept moving at all times and never be stationary on the work. Remember to concentrate on the edges and corners – the centre of the work will take care of itself. Remember that only practice will tell you how much pressure is needed on the pad at any given time.

OIL FINISH

As with wax, there are several recipes for oil finishes, one of which is, one part cold-drawn linseed oil to be simmered for ten minutes and then strained through a cotton rag. One eighth turpentine is then added and thoroughly mixed over a low heat. The oil is applied daily over the course of five or six weeks, being well rubbed into the timber and any excess oil wiped off. Before the next application of oil the surface is washed with cold water to remove any dirt or dust. An oil finish can take time and effort, but in the end you will have an authentic finish that is hard wearing and easy to maintain. Liberon Waxes produce a finishing oil that is ideal and much quicker and easier to use than linseed oil.

TABLE-TOP POLISH

Table top polish can be obtained from Fiddes Polishing supplies in Cardiff, and is a clear polish that can be applied with a polishing mop. When dry it is impervious to water and spirit. Two or three coats can be applied, rubbing down lightly between coats with fine paper or 0000 wire wool. The polish takes seven days to harden off, after which time it can be lightly rubbed down and waxed or, if the grain has been filled, it can be rubbed down to a perfectly flat surface and a high gloss can be obtained by burnishing the surface with a burnishing cream.

POLYURETHANE

There are various types of polyurethane polish on the market that can be applied with a brush. These can be allowed to harden off completely and then be rubbed down and burnished with a preparatory burnishing cream which is obtainable from polishing suppliers. Follow the instructions on the tin.

INDEX